WRITERS ON WRITING

SECOND EDITION

Selected and compiled by
Jon Winokur

RUNNING PRESS
Philadelphia, Pennsylvania

Canadian representatives: General Publishing Co., Ltd., 30 Lesmill Road, Don Mills,
Ontario M3B 2T6. International representatives: Worldwide Media Services, Inc., 115
East 23rd Street, New York, NY 10010.

9   8   7   6   5   4   3   2   1
Digit on the right indicates the number of this printing.

Library of Congress Cataloging in Publication Data:
Writers on writing.
Includes index.
        1. Authorship—Quotations, maxims, etc.   2. Authors—
Quotations. I. Winokur, Jon.
PN165.W68 1987 808.88'2 86-31462
ISBN 0-89471-522-4 (Cloth)

Printed by Port City Press, Baltimore
Cover design by Toby Schmidt
Typography: Paladium by rci, Philadelphia, Copperplate Gothic by Letraset

This book may be ordered by mail from the publisher.
Please include $1.50 for postage.
But try your bookstore first!
Running Press Book Publishers
125 South 22nd Street
Philadelphia, Pennsylvania 19103

Acknowledgments

I'm grateful to Lawrence Teacher and Stuart Teacher
of Running Press for their extraordinary commitment to this book.
I wish to thank Melissa Cookman, Dorothy Hoffman,
Cynthia Johnson, Nancy Lea Johnson, Howard LeNoble,
Anita Nelson, Susan Nethery, Toby Schmidt, Laurie Schlesinger,
Steve Schuhle, Nancy Steele, Frank Zachary, Steve Zorn,
and Elizabeth Zozom for their invaluable help.
I'm indebted to Tobi Sanders, Linda Takahashi, and Mark Wolgin
for their support and good counsel.

For Skip and Elinor

CONTENTS

CONTENTS

INTRODUCTION

I love quotations. Maybe it's a symptom of a short-attention-span, instant-gratification age, but I'm a sucker for a well stated tidbit of brevity and wit. For me, quotes do with precision what reading does in general: they confirm the astuteness of my perceptions, they open the way to ideas, and they console me with the knowledge that I'm not alone.

I began collecting quotes on writing at the age of seventeen, when I first had the notion to be a writer. I was fascinated with the creative process and curious about writing as an occupation. I wanted to know why and how and when and where they do it. I wanted to know what it *takes* to be a writer.

Fortunately, most writers love to talk about it.

They're full of advice to young writers, prescriptions for success and failure, and tips on dealing with demon publishers. They philosophize about Art and posit definitions of Style. They have opinions on censorship, plagiarism, and the need to revise. They speculate on the role of alcohol in the production of literature and declare why they write. They divulge such trade secrets as how to plan a novel and how to handle an editor. They gossip about colleagues and grapple with the terror of the blank page. They lament the agony of rejection. They feel guilty when they don't write. They discuss their characters as if they were real people, and they get even with critics.

They talk about talking about writing.

And above all, they reveal their talent, dedication and humanity.

Here, then, the result of twenty years of compulsive collecting, to be read for amusement, for reference, or out of sheer fascination with the writer's art.

WRITERS AND
WRITING

The writer . . . is a person who talks to himself, or better, who talks in himself.
Malcolm Cowley

The writer is the Faust of modern society, the only surviving individualist in a mass age. To his orthodox contemporaries he seems a semi-madman.
Boris Pasternak

A writer is a reader who is moved to emulation.
William Maxwell

A writer is someone who always sells. An author is one who writes a book that makes a big splash.
Mickey Spillane

A writer is someone who can make a riddle out of an answer.
Karl Kraus

A writer is not someone who expresses his thoughts, his passion or his imagination in sentences but someone who thinks sentences. A Sentence-Thinker.
Roland Barthes

A writer wastes nothing.
F. Scott Fitzgerald

I think you must remember that a writer is a simple-minded person to begin with and go on that basis. He's not a great mind, he's not a great thinker, he's not a great philosopher, he's a storyteller.
Erskine Caldwell

Every writer is a frustrated actor who recites his lines in the hidden auditorium of his skull.
Rod Serling

There is only one trait that marks the writer. He is always watching. It's a kind of trick of mind and he is born with it.
Morley Callaghan

The role of the writer is not to say what we can all say, but what we are unable to say.
Anaïs Nin

Writers are self-indulgent, full of self-pity, forever seeking reassurance, constantly occupied with what they consider the proper conditions of work, and the next thing to invalids in their demands upon life.
  Delmore Schwartz

Writers are always selling somebody out.
  Joan Didion

My belief is that all authors are essentially lonely men. Every one of them has to do his work in a room alone, and he inevitably gets very tired of himself.
  H.L. Mencken

A writer is essentially a man who does not resign himself to loneliness.
  François Mauriac

Most writers are in a state of gloom a good deal of the time; they need perpetual reassurance.
  John Hall Wheelock

Most writers had unhappy childhoods.
  Judith Krantz

There are two kinds of writers, those who are and those who aren't. With the first, content and form belong together like soul and body; with the second, they match each other like body and clothes.
  Karl Kraus

Writers, like teeth, are divided into incisors and grinders.
  Walter Bagehot

A writer's mind seems to be situated partly in the solar plexus and partly in the head.
  Ethel Wilson

The true function of a writer is to produce a masterpiece and . . . no other task is of any consequence.
  Cyril Connolly

Writers can treat their mental illnesses every day.
  Kurt Vonnegut

Writers shouldn't propound their own theories. They should do what painters do: Get their wives, husbands, or old school chums to write the manifestoes.
  Tom Wolfe

There is no way of being a creative writer in America without being a loser.
  Nelson Algren

Our society, like decadent Rome, has turned into an amusement society, with writers chief among the court jesters—not so much above the clatter as part of it.
  Saul Bellow

Among European writers you may distinguish the bad one from the good one by the simple fact that the bad one has generally one nightingale at a time, as happens in conventional poetry, while the good one has several of them sing together, as they really do in nature.
  Vladimir Nabokov

American writers never have a second act.
  F. Scott Fitzgerald

In America only the successful writer is important, in France all writers are important, in England no writer is important, in Australia you have to explain what a writer is.
  Geoffrey Cotterell

English authors write better than Americans—and Irish authors write better than anybody.
  Dorothy Parker

The Jewish writer suffers from the unavailability of a sufficient variety of observed experience. He is forced to write, if he is serious, the way the pelican feeds its young, striking his own breast to draw the blood of his theme.
  Clement Greenberg

Whenever citizens are seen routinely as enemies of their own government, writers are routinely seen to be the most dangerous enemies.
  E.L. Doctorow

For a country to have a great writer is like having a second government. That is why no regime has ever loved great writers, only minor ones.
  Alexander Solzhenitsyn

The writer, like the priest, must be exempted from secular labor. His work needs a frolic health; he must be at the top of his condition.
  Ralph Waldo Emerson

The writer must be able to see where he was lying to himself, where his mouth was full of sawdust instead of grapes, where his gunpowder was only snuff.
  Peter Straub

Everything goes by the board: honor, pride, decency . . . to get the book written. If a writer has to rob his mother, he will not hesitate; the "Ode on a Grecian Urn" is worth any number of old ladies.
  William Faulkner

No wonder the really powerful men in our society, whether politicians or scientists, hold writers and poets in contempt. They do it because they get no evidence from modern literature that anybody is thinking about any significant question.
  Saul Bellow

I am convinced that all writers are optimists whether they concede the point or not ... How otherwise could any human being sit down to a pile of blank sheets and decide to write, say two hundred thousand words on a given theme?
    Thomas Costain

There are other writers who would persuade you not to go on, that everything is nonsense, that you should kill yourself. They, of course, go on to write another book while you have killed yourself.
    John Gardner

Writers are interesting people, but often mean and petty.
    Lillian Hellman

To me a writer is one of the most important soldiers in the fight for the survival of the human race. He must stay at his post in the thick of fire to serve the cause of mankind.
    Leon Uris

Many people who want to be writers don't really want to be writers. They want to *have been* writers. They wish they had a book in print.
    James Michener

Good writers are monotonous, like good composers. Their truth is self-repeating ... They keep trying to perfect their understanding of the one problem they were born to understand.
    Alberto Moravia

Good writers define reality, bad ones merely restate it. A good writer turns fact into truth; a bad writer will, more often than not, accomplish the opposite.
    Edward Albee

What I like in a good author is not what he says, but what he whispers.
    Logan Pearsall Smith

A great writer creates a world of his own and his readers are proud to live in it. A lesser writer may entice them in for a moment, but soon he will watch them filing out.
    Cyril Connolly

Great writers are always evil influences; second-rate writers are not wicked enough to become great.
    George Bernard Shaw

Screenwriters are like little gypsies swimming in an aquarium filled with sharks, killer whales, squid, octopuses and other creatures of the deep. And plenty of squid shit.
    Joseph Wambaugh

We romantic writers are there to make people feel and not think.
    Barbara Cartland

When one says that a writer is fashionable one practically always means that he is admired by people under thirty.
  George Orwell

He is a writer for the ages—the ages of four to eight.
  Dorothy Parker

The South has produced writers as the Dark Ages produced saints.
  Alfred Kazin

Why has the South produced so many good writers? Because we got beat.
  Walker Percy

When I'm asked why Southern writers particularly have a penchant for writing about freaks, I say it's because we are still able to recognize one.
  Flannery O'Connor

Being a writer in the South has its special miseries, which include isolation, madness, tics, amnesia, alcoholism, lust, and loss of ordinary powers of speech. One may go for days without saying a word.
  Walker Percy

Being a Southern writer is a decision, not a fate.
  Elizabeth Hardwick

What no wife of a writer can ever understand is that a writer is working when he's staring out the window.
  Burton Rascoe

If, as Dr. Johnson said, a man who is not married is only half a man, so a man who is very much married is only half a writer.
  Cyril Connolly

Pretty women swarm around everybody but writers. Plain, intelligent women *somewhat*, swarm around writers.
  William Saroyan

Writers age more quickly than athletes.
  Tennessee Williams

A writer has nothing to say after the age of forty; if he is clever he knows how to hide it.
  Georges Simenon

If you're a singer, you lose your voice. A baseball player loses his arm. A writer gets more knowledge, and if he's good, the older he gets, the better he writes.
  Mickey Spillane

I am more interested in works than in authors.
  E.M. Forster

I get very tired of reading about writers. I don't even understand why people want to read novels about them. There's apparently some glamour, but I'll be damned if I can see it. I would much rather try to understand the lives of people who don't write letters to the *New York Review of Books*.
  Rosellen Brown

So-called "serious" writers only write about writers writing stories about writers writing stories.
Ian Shoales

The best part of every author is in general to be found in his book, I assure you.
Samuel Johnson

The life of a writer has always seemed to me to be about as good a one as a low human being could hope for.
George Jean Nathan

Writers . . . live over-strained lives in which far too much humanity is sacrificed to far too little art.
Raymond Chandler

There is no denying the fact that writers should be read but not seen. Rarely are they a winsome sight.
Edna Ferber

Authors are like cattle going to a fair: those of the same field can never move on without butting one another.
Walter Savage Landor

Authors are sometimes like tomcats: they distrust all the other toms, but they are kind to kittens.
Malcolm Cowley

Most writers . . . are awful sticks to talk with.
Sherwood Anderson

No complete son of a bitch ever wrote a good sentence.
Malcolm Cowley

Every asshole in the world wants to write.
Judith Rossner

No author ever spared a brother;
Wits and gamecocks to one another.
John Gay

Never believe anything a writer tells you about himself. A man comes to believe in the end the lies he tells himself about himself.
George Bernard Shaw

I don't like writers.
May Sarton

We are all apprentices in a craft where no one ever becomes a master.
Ernest Hemingway

It all began with the first storyteller of the tribe. He began to put forth words, not because he thought others might reply with other predictable words, but to test the extent to which words could fit with one another, give birth to one another—in order to extract an explanation of the world from the thread of every possible spoken narrative, and from the arabesque that nouns and verbs, subjects and predicates performed as they unfolded from one another.
Italo Calvino

Writing is turning one's worst moments into money.
J.P. Donleavy

Writing's an important way of living.
William Burroughs

Writing is a form of self-flagellation.
William Styron

Writing is an act of ego.
William Zinsser

Writing is a struggle against silence.
Carlos Fuentes

To write is in some way to cut the seemingly automatic pattern of violence, destructiveness, and death wish. To write is to put the seeming insignificance of human existence into a different perspective. It is the need, the wish, and, please God, the ability, to reorder our physical faith.
Alfred Kazin

All writing is pigshit. People who come out of nowhere to try to put into words any part of what goes on in their minds are pigs.
Antonin Artaud

To write is to kill something to death.
Jean Cocteau

Writing is busy idleness.
Goethe

The act of writing is an act of optimism. You would not take the trouble to do it if you felt that it didn't matter.
Edward Albee

Writing is: the science of the various blisses of language.
Roland Barthes

Writing is a dog's life, but the only life worth living.
Gustave Flaubert

Writing's not terrible, it's wonderful. I keep my own hours, do what I please. When I want to travel, I can. But mainly I'm doing what I most wanted to do all my life. I'm not into the agonies of creation.
Raymond Carver

Writing is so much damned fun. I play God. I feel like a kid at Christmas. I make people do what I want, and I change things as I go along.
    Tom Clancy

I love being a writer. What I can't stand is the paperwork.
    Peter De Vries

The desire to write grows with writing.
    Erasmus

Anything that isn't writing is easy.
    Jimmy Breslin

I have always been able to gain my living without doing any work; for the writing of books and magazine matter was always play, not work. I enjoyed it; it was merely billiards to me.
    Mark Twain

To practice art in order to earn money, flatter the public, spin facetious or dismal yarns for reputation or cash—that is the most ignoble of professions.
    Gustave Flaubert

Writing is a yoga that invokes Lord mind.
    Allen Ginsberg

Writing is making sense of life.
    Nadine Gordimer

Writing is putting one's obsessions in order.
    Jean Grenier

Writing is a suspension of life in order to re-create life.
    John McPhee

Writing is like manual labor of the mind: a job, like laying pipe.
    John Gregory Dunne

Writing is the hardest work in the world not involving heavy lifting.
    Pete Hamill

I do not like to write, for the simple reason that writing is extremely hard work, and I do not "like" extremely hard work.
    William F. Buckley, Jr.

Writing is one of the few professions left where you take all the responsibility for what you do. It's really dangerous and ultimately destroys you as a writer if you start thinking about responses to your work or what your audience needs.
    Erica Jong

Writing is no trouble: you just jot down ideas as they occur to you. The jotting is simplicity itself—it is the occurring which is difficult.
    Stephen Leacock

Planning to write is not writing. Outlining a book is not writing. Researching is not writing. Talking to people about what you're doing, none of that is writing. Writing is writing.
> *E.L. Doctorow*

To write is to inform against others.
> *Violette Leduc*

I love writing. I love the swirl and swing of words as they tangle with human emotions.
> *James Michener*

I hate writing. I will do anything to avoid it. The only way I could write less was if I was dead.
> *Fran Lebowitz*

Writing, like life itself, is a voyage of discovery.
> *Henry Miller*

Writing is a very silly business at best. There is a certain ridiculousness about putting down a picture of life. Oh, it's a real horse's ass business. The mountain labors and groans and strains and the tiniest of rodents comes out.
> *John Steinbeck*

Writing doesn't get easier with experience. The more you know, the harder it is to write.
> *Tim O'Brien*

You can recover from the writing malady only by falling mortally ill and dying.
> *Jules Renard*

Writing is just having a sheet of paper, a pen and not a shadow of an idea of what you're going to say.
> *Françoise Sagan*

To hold a pen is to be at war.
> *Voltaire*

The pen is worse than the sword.
> *Robert Burton*

The pen is a formidable weapon, but a man can kill himself with it a great deal more easily than he can other people.
> *George Dennison Prentice*

There is no lighter burden, nor more agreeable, than a pen.
> *Petrarch*

When I stepped from hard manual work to writing, I just stepped from one kind of hard work to another.
> *Sean O'Casey*

Writing a book is like driving a car at night. You only see as far as your headlights go, but you can make the whole trip that way.
> *E.L. Doctorow*

To me, writing is a horseback ride into heaven and hell and back. I am grateful if I can crawl back alive.
   Thomas Sanchez

Writing is not a profession, occupation or job; it is not a way of life: it is a comprehensive response to life.
   Gregory McDonald

The great art of writing is the art of making people real to themselves with words.
   Logan Pearsall Smith

The craft or art of writing is the clumsy attempt to find symbols for the wordlessness. In utter loneliness a writer tries to explain the inexplicable.
   John Steinbeck

Often I think writing is a sheer paring away of oneself leaving always something thinner, barer, more meager.
   F. Scott Fitzgerald

Great writing has been a staff to lean on, a mother to consult, a wisdom to pick up stumbling folly, a strength in weakness and a courage to support sick cowardice.
   John Steinbeck

Writing ... keeps me from believing everything I read.
   Gloria Steinem

For me, writing is the only thing that passes the three tests of *métier*: (1) when I'm doing it, I don't feel that I should be doing something else instead; (2) it produces a sense of accomplishment and, once in a while, pride; and (3) it's frightening.
   Gloria Steinem

Writing, when properly managed (as you may be sure I think mine is), is but a different name for conversation.
   Laurence Sterne

This is what I find most encouraging about the writing trades: They allow mediocre people who are patient and industrious to revise their stupidity, to edit themselves into something like intelligence. They also allow lunatics to seem saner than sane.
   Kurt Vonnegut

What is wrong with most writing today is its flaccidity, its lack of pleasure in the manipulation of sounds and pauses. The written word is becoming inert. One dreads to think what it will be like in 2020.
   Anthony Burgess

The purpose of writing is to hold a mirror to nature, but too much today is written from small mirrors in vanity cases.
   John Mason Brown

All writing is communication; creative writing is communication through revelation—it is the self escaping into the open. No writer long remains incognito.
   E.B. White

Incessant scribbling is death to thought.
   Thomas Carlyle

When I'm not writing, I don't think.
   E.L. Doctorow

Writing is incompatible with everything.
   Paul Theroux

Writers don't have lifestyles. They sit in little rooms and write.
   Norman Mailer

If I didn't have writing, I'd be running down the street hurling grenades in people's faces.
   Paul Fussell

This sickness, to express oneself. What is it?
   Jean Cocteau

An insane life, but what happiness!
   William Maxwell

MOTIVES AND
ASPIRATIONS

The writer has a grudge against society, which he documents with
accounts of unsatisfying sex, unrealized ambition, unmitigated loneliness,
and a sense of local and global distress.
  Renata Adler

Every author really wants to have letters printed in the papers. Unable to
make the grade, he drops down a rung of the ladder and writes novels.
  P.G. Wodehouse

Writing a book is such a complicated, long-term, difficult process that all
of the possible motives that can funnel in will, and a great many of those
motives will be base. If you can transform your particular baseness into
something beautiful, that's about the best you can make of your own
obnoxious nature.
  William Gass

I do think that the quality which makes a man want to write and be read
is essentially a desire for self-exposure and is masochistic. Like one of those
guys who has a compulsion to take his thing out and show it on the
street.
  James Jones

Writers, if they are worthy of that jealous designation, do not write for
other writers. They write to give reality to experience.
  Archibald MacLeish

All writers are vain, selfish, and lazy, and at the very bottom of their
motives there lies a mystery. Writing a book is a horrible, exhausting
struggle, like a long bout of some painful illness. One would never undertake such a thing if one were not driven on by some demon whom one
can neither resist nor understand. For all one knows that demon is simply
the same instinct that makes a baby squall for attention.
  George Orwell

There are three reasons for becoming a writer: the first is that you need
the money; the second, that you have something to say that you think the
world should know; the third is that you can't think what to do with the
long winter evenings.
  Quentin Crisp

Why had I become a writer in the first place? Because I wasn't fit for society; I didn't fit into the system.
Brian Aldiss

I write to ease the passing of time.
Jorge Luis Borges

The number one reason why any professional writer writes is to pay the bills. This isn't the Lawn Tennis Association where you play just for the thrill of it.
Jimmy Breslin

I write because I hate. A lot. Hard.
William Gass

You write because you want to be read. But you want to be read on your own terms.
William Styron

You don't write because you want to say something; you write because you've got something to say.
F. Scott Fitzgerald

I write books to find out about things.
Rebecca West

Word and substance—that is the only connection I have striven for in my life.
Karl Kraus

They ask me if I were on a desert island and knew nobody would ever see what I wrote, would I go on writing. My answer is most emphatically yes, I would go on writing for company. Because I'm creating an imaginary— it's always imaginary—world in which I would like to live.
William Burroughs

I'm not one of those writers you'll hear say, "When you are a writer, you never retire, you go on writing—that's your life." Living is my life. I write in order to stay alive.
Quentin Crisp

I feel a need to have a certain experience, to see certain feelings displayed, to see certain ideas pursued, and at one point or another I make the audacious choice of appointing myself as the person who can conceivably do that.
Scott Spencer

My father said I was the ugliest child he had ever seen. He told me that all his life and I believed him. And I'd accepted that nobody would ever love me. But do you know, nobody cares what a writer looks like. I could write to be eighty and be as grotesque as a dwarf and that wouldn't matter. For me, writing was an act of love. It was an attempt not to get the world's attention, it was an attempt to be loved.
James Baldwin

I started writing because of a terrible feeling of powerlessness: I felt I was drifting and obscure, and I rebelled against that. I didn't see what I could do to change my condition. I wanted to control rather than be controlled, to ordain rather than be ordained, and to relegate rather than be relegated.
   Anita Brookner

I revel in the prospect of being able to torture a phrase once more.
   S.J. Perelman

How do I know what I think until I see what I say?
   E.M. Forster

Writers write to influence their readers, their preachers, their auditors, but always, at bottom, to be more themselves.
   Aldous Huxley

There are many reasons why novelists write, but they all have one thing in common: a need to create an alternative world.
   John Fowles

My purpose is to entertain myself first and other people secondly.
   John D. MacDonald

My task is by the power of the written word to make you hear, to make you feel—it is, before all, to make you see.
   Joseph Conrad

I write in order to attain that feeling of tension relieved and function achieved which a cow enjoys on giving milk.
   H.L. Mencken

The only reason for being a professional writer is that you just can't help it.
   Leo Rosten

I have always been in a condition in which I cannot *not* write.
   Barbara Tuchman

I can say now that one of the big reasons was this: I instinctively recognized an opportunity to transcend some of my personal failings—things about myself I didn't particularly like and wanted to change but didn't know how.
   John Steinbeck

I've never had "ideas" about poetry. To me it's always been a personal, almost physical release or solution to a complex pressure of needs—wanting to create, to justify, to praise, to externalize, depending on the circumstances. And I've never been much interested in other people's poetry—one reason for writing, of course, is that no one's written what you want to read.
   Philip Larkin

I write fiction because it's a way of making statements I can disown. I write plays because dialogue is the most respectable way of contradicting myself.
   Tom Stoppard

No man would set a word down on paper if he had the courage to live out what he believed in.
Henry Miller

The physical business of writing is unpleasant to me, but the psychic satisfaction of discharging bad ideas in worse English makes me forget it.
H.L. Mencken

One writes to find words' meanings.
Joy Williams

Getting even is one reason for writing.
William Gass

I am often asked why I write, and I don't know really—I just want to.
John Ashbery

If you ask me what I came to do in this world, I, an artist, I will answer you: I am here to live out loud.
Émile Zola

I shall live badly if I do not write, and I shall write badly if I do not live.
Françoise Sagan

If I don't write, I'll die.
James T. Farrell

If I could think, maybe I wouldn't write.
Scott Spencer

I don't want to be a doctor, and live by men's diseases; nor a minister to live by their sins; nor a lawyer to live by their quarrels. So I don't see there's anything left for me but to be an author.
Nathaniel Hawthorne

My main reason for adopting literature as a profession was that, as the author is never seen by his clients, he need not dress respectably.
George Bernard Shaw

I wanted to be a man of the world and I took to writing as I might have taken to archaeology or diplomacy or any other profession, as a means of coming to terms with the world. Now I see it as an end in itself.
Evelyn Waugh

A writer is someone who writes, that's all. You can't stop it; you can't make yourself do anything else but that.
Gore Vidal

I love to tell stories.
Irving Wallace

The writer's intention hasn't anything to do with what he achieves. The intent to earn money or the intent to be famous or the intent to be great doesn't matter in the end. Just what comes out.
Lillian Hellman

I wrote a short story because I wanted to see something of mine in print, other than my fingers.
  Wilson Mizner

I want to write the story that will zero in and give you intense, but not connected, moments of experience. I guess that's the way I see life. People remake themselves bit by bit and do things they don't understand.
  Alice Munro

I wrote my first novel because I wanted to read it.
  Toni Morrison

At the time of writing, I don't write for my friends or myself, either; I write for *it*, for the pleasure of *it*.
  Eudora Welty

If you can't annoy somebody, there is little point in writing.
  Kingsley Amis

On the whole, I don't want to think too much about why I write what I write. If I know what I'm doing . . . I can't do it.
  Joan Didion

What I am trying to achieve is a voice sitting by a fireplace telling you a story on a winter's evening.
  Truman Capote

What I want is to possess my readers while they are reading my book—if I can, to possess them in ways that other writers don't.
  Philip Roth

Unless one is a genius, it is best to aim at being intelligible.
  Anthony Hope Hawkins

A writer's problem does not change. He himself changes and the world he lives in changes but his problem remains the same. It is always how to write truly and having found what is true, to project it in such a way that it becomes part of the experience of the person who reads it.
  Ernest Hemingway

There is one thing that matters—to set a chime of words tinkling in the minds of a few fastidious people.
  Logan Pearsall Smith

Any writer overwhelmingly honest about pleasing himself is almost sure to please others.
  Marianne Moore

I never wanted to grow up to be a writer, I just wanted to grow up to be an adult.
  Toni Morrison

I never deliberately set out to shock, but when people don't walk out of my plays I think there is something wrong.
  John Osborne

The sour truth is that I am imprisoned with a perception which will settle for nothing less than making a revolution in the consciousness of our time.
Norman Mailer

I'm writing to have fun and for my readers to have fun. I do the best work I can do.
Judith Krantz

Anything that is written to please the author is worthless.
Blaise Pascal

The writer who aims at producing the platitudes which are "not for an age but for all time" has his reward in being unreadable in all ages.
George Bernard Shaw

It is my ambition to say in ten sentences what other men say in whole books—what other men do *not* say in whole books.
Friedrich Wilhelm Nietzsche

I am trying—in a good cause—to crowd people out of their own minds and occupy their space. I want them to stop being themselves for the moment, I want them to stop thinking, and I want to occupy their heads. I want to use language and I want the language to reverberate and I want to use the white spaces between the lines.
Robert Stone

What I want to do is make people laugh so they'll see things seriously.
William Zinsser

I want to write the words that people want to print.
Quentin Crisp

I want to be the Minnesota Fats of science fiction.
Frank Herbert

I intend to become America's black female Proust.
Maya Angelou

I want to entertain people by the millions.
Mickey Spillane

I have tried simply to write the best I can; sometimes I have good luck and write better than I can.
Ernest Hemingway

A book is produced by the whole man, who is more complicated than any other single object in the universe, and its motivation is therefore just as mysterious and ineluctable.
William Golding

Whence, if ever, shall come the actuality
Of a voice speaking the mind's knowing,
The sunlight bright on the green windowshade,
And the self articulate, affectionate, and flowing,
Ease, warmth, light, the utter showing,
When in the white bed all things are made.
    Delmore Schwartz

I always wanted to write a book that ended with the word *mayonnaise*.
    Richard Brautigan

ART AND
THE ARTIST

All art is concerned with coming into being.
    Aristotle

I feel that art has something to do with the achievement of stillness in the midst of chaos. A stillness which characterizes prayer, too, and the eye of the storm. I think that art has something to do with an arrest of attention in the midst of distraction.
    Saul Bellow

Art is a vision of heaven gratuitously given.
    Anthony Burgess

Art is nature speeded up and God slowed down.
    Malcolm De Chazal

Art is life seen through a temperament.
    Émile Zola

All art is a struggle to be, in a particular sort of way, virtuous.
    Iris Murdoch

All art is a revolt against man's fate.
    André Malraux

Art is the apotheosis of solitude.
    Samuel Beckett

Art is an attempt to integrate evil.
    Simone de Beauvoir

After all, art is a form of entertainment, yes? For both the maker and the consumer.
    Raymond Carver

The art of art, the glory of expression and the sunshine of the light of letters is simplicity.
    Walt Whitman

Art never initiates. It merely takes over what is already present in the real world and makes an aesthetic pattern out of it, or tries to explain it, or tries to relate it to some other aspect of life.
    Anthony Burgess

The difference between Art and Life is that Art is more bearable.
   Charles Bukowski

We have art in order not to die of the truth.
   Friedrich Wilhelm Nietzsche

Art, like morality, consists in drawing the line somewhere.
   G.K. Chesterton

In art, as in love, instinct is enough.
   Anatole France

The containment of our confusions is what we call sanity. The resolution
of confusions, the painstaking removal of the stew's ingredients and the
remaking of a better stew is what we call art.
   Geoffrey Wolff

Art is a marriage of the conscious and the unconscious.
   Jean Cocteau

Beauty plus pity—that is the closest we can get to a definition of art.
   Vladimir Nabokov

A work that aspires, however humbly, to the condition of art should carry
its justification in every line.
   Joseph Conrad

A tale charms by its ingenuity, by the plausibility with which it overcomes
the suspicion that it couldn't happen. That is art.
   Jacques Barzun

To reveal art and conceal the artist is art's aim.
   Oscar Wilde

To make us feel small in the right way is a function of art. Men can only
make us feel small in the wrong way.
   E.M. Forster

Nothing I wrote saved a single Jew from being gassed . . . it's perfectly all
right to be an *engagé* writer as long as you don't think you're changing
things. Art is our chief means of breaking bread with the dead.
   W.H. Auden

The work of art is an idea that one exaggerates.
   André Gide

A great work of art is a kind of suicide.
   Al Alvarez

Art is uncompromising, and life is full of compromises.
   Günter Grass

There's no "Safety First" in Art.
   F. Scott Fitzgerald

Art-speech is the only truth. An artist is usually a damned liar, but his art,
if it be art, will tell you the truth of his day.
   D.H. Lawrence

Art for art's sake makes no more sense than gin for gin's sake.
W. Somerset Maugham

Art is only a means to life, to the life more abundant. It merely points
the way.
Henry Miller

Life is very nice, but it lacks form. It's the aim of art to give it some.
Jean Anouilh

Life, the raw material, is only lived *in potentia* until the artist deploys it in
his work.
Lawrence Durrell

The most important thing in a work of art is that it should have a kind of
focus, i.e., there should be some place where all the rays meet or from
which they issue. And this focus must not be able to be completely
explained by words.
Leo Tolstoy

A work of art has no importance whatever to society. It is only important
to the individual.
Vladimir Nabokov

It is the function of art to renew our perception. What we are familiar
with we cease to see. The writer shakes up the familiar scene, and as if by
magic, we see a new meaning in it.
Anaïs Nin

Art is a form of catharsis.
Dorothy Parker

Art is the reasoned derangement of the senses.
Kenneth Rexroth

In everything that can be called art there is a quality of redemption.
It may be pure tragedy, if it is high tragedy, and it may be pity and irony,
and it may be the raucous laughter of the strong man. But down these
mean streets a man must go who is not himself mean, who is neither tar-
nished nor afraid. The detective in this kind of story must be such a man.
Raymond Chandler

Art must take reality by surprise.
Françoise Sagan

Art is like a border of flowers along the course of civilization.
Lincoln Steffens

Without art, the crudeness of reality would make the world unbearable.
George Bernard Shaw

Without freedom, no art; art lives only on the restraint it imposes on
itself, and dies of all others.
Albert Camus

Art is simpler than people think because there is so little to write about. All the moving things are eternal in man's history and have been written before, and if a man writes hard enough, sincerely enough, and with the unalterable determination never, never to be quite satisfied with it he will repeat them because art, like poverty, takes care of its own, shares its bread.
   William Faulkner

A work of art is not a matter of thinking beautiful thoughts or experiencing tender emotions (though those are its raw materials) but of intelligence, skill, taste, proportion, knowledge, discipline and industry; especially discipline.
   Evelyn Waugh

It depends little on the object, much on the mood, in art.
   Ralph Waldo Emerson

Emotion resulting from a work of art is only of value when it is not obtained by sentimental blackmail.
   Jean Cocteau

All art has this characteristic—it unites people.
   Leo Tolstoy

Art raises its head where creeds relax.
   Friedrich Wilhelm Nietzsche

In Art, the public accept what has been, because they cannot alter it, not because they appreciate it. They swallow their classics whole, and never taste them.
   Oscar Wilde

All good art is indiscretion.
   Tennessee Williams

All art is quite useless.
   Oscar Wilde

My first thought about art, as a child, was that the artist brings something into the world that didn't exist before, and that he does it without destroying something else. A kind of refutation of the conservation of matter. That still seems to me its central magic, its core of joy.
   John Updike

Art distills sensation and embodies it with enhanced meaning in memorable form—or else it is not art.
   Jacques Barzun

The artist is of no importance. Only what he creates is important, since there is nothing new to be said.
   William Faulkner

Artists can color the sky red because they know it's blue. Those of us who aren't artists must color things the way they really are or people might think we're stupid.
   Jules Feiffer

The vanity of the artist is of a very curious nature because it is tied to death. Trying to cheat it. And all perfect nonsense, but it fills the days.
Gore Vidal

You can only be an artist if you've been up to a point lucky with your background and put in years of reading; you can't step off the factory conveyor-belt and do it.
Martin Amis

The artist produces for the liberation of his soul. It is his nature to create as it is the nature of water to run down hill.
W. Somerset Maugham

An artist must be a reactionary. He has to stand out against the tenor of the age and not go flopping along.
Evelyn Waugh

The task which the artist implicitly sets himself is to overthrow existing values, to make of the chaos about him an order which is his own, to sow strife and ferment so that by the emotional release those who are dead may be restored to life.
Henry Miller

All artists are two-headed calves.
Truman Capote

The true artist is the person who never takes anything for granted.
Vladimir Nabokov

The true artist declares himself by leaving out a lot. The artist alone sees spirits. But after he has told of their appearing to him, everybody sees them.
Goethe

The artist, like the God of creation, remains within or behind or beyond or above his handiwork, invisible, refined, out of existence, indifferent, paring his fingernails.
James Joyce

The artist should be in his work like God in creation, invisible and all-powerful; he should be felt everywhere and seen nowhere.
Gustave Flaubert

The better the artist, the more vulnerable he seems to be.
Al Alvarez

An artist cannot speak about his art any more than a plant can discuss horticulture.
Jean Cocteau

When those old writing boys get to talking about The Artist, meaning themselves, I want to leave the profession.
John Steinbeck

READERS AND READING

He is so stupid you can't trust him with an idea.
He is so clever he will catch you in the least error.
He will not buy short books.
He will not buy long books.
He is part moron, part genius and part ogre.
There is some doubt as to whether he can read.
  John Steinbeck

No one can write decently who is distrustful of the reader's intelligence, or whose attitude is patronizing.
  E.B. White

The natural habit of any good and critical reader is to disbelieve what you are telling him and try to escape out of the world you are picturing.
  Angus Wilson

Those who write clearly have readers; those who write obscurely have commentators.
  Albert Camus

Someone says, "Whom do you write for?" I reply: "Do you read me?" If they say, "Yes," I say, "Do you like it?" If they say, "No," then I say, "I don't write for you."
  W.H. Auden

I have no fans. You know what I got? Customers.
  Mickey Spillane

Books give not wisdom where was none before,
But where some is, there reading makes it more.
  John Harington

If there's one major cause for the spread of mass illiteracy, it's the fact that everybody can read and write.
  Peter De Vries

The ratio of literacy to illiteracy is constant, but nowadays the illiterates can read.
  Alberto Moravia

People don't like using dictionaries when they're reading mere novels.
   Anthony Burgess

Books must be read as deliberately and reservedly as they were written.
   Henry David Thoreau

A great many people now reading and writing would be better employed keeping rabbits.
   Edith Sitwell

In anything fit to be called by the name of reading, the process itself should be absorbing and voluptuous; we should gloat over a book, be rapt clean out of ourselves.
   Robert Louis Stevenson

'Tis the good reader that makes the good book.
   Ralph Waldo Emerson

In relation to a writer, most readers believe in the Double Standard: they may be unfaithful to him as often as they like, but he must never, never be unfaithful to them.
   W.H. Auden

I think the writer ought to help the reader as much as he can without damaging what he wants to say; and I don't think it ever hurts the writer to sort of stand back now and then and look at his stuff as if he were reading it instead of writing it.
   James Jones

He who does not expect a million readers should not write a line.
   Goethe

A writer's ambition should be to trade a hundred contemporary readers for ten readers in ten years' time and one reader in a hundred years' time.
   Arthur Koestler

There are some people who read too much: the bibliobibuli. I know some who are constantly drunk on books, as other men are drunk on whiskey or religion. They wander through this most diverting and stimulating of worlds in a haze, seeing nothing and hearing nothing.
   H.L. Mencken

People who don't read are brutes.
   Eugène Ionesco

I divide all readers into two classes; those who read to remember and those who read to forget.
   William Lyon Phelps

An author ought to write for the youth of his own generation, the critics of the next, and the schoolmasters of ever afterward.
   F. Scott Fitzgerald

I don't have a sense of a so-called ideal reader and certainly not of a readership, that terrific entity. I write for the page.
   Don DeLillo

All great men have written proudly, nor cared to explain. They knew that the intelligent reader would come at last, and would thank them.
Ralph Waldo Emerson

When I'm writing I'm always aware that this friend is going to like this, or that another friend is going to like that paragraph or chapter, always thinking of specific people. In the end all books are written for your friends.
Gabriel Garcia Márquez

I don't think I've ever written anything that is designed purely as a sop to the reader: I don't put in bits of sex to increase sales. But I always bear him in mind, and try to visualize him and watch for any signs of boredom or impatience to flit across the face of this rather shadowy being, the Reader.
Kingsley Amis

The ideal reader of my novels is a lapsed Catholic and failed musician, short-sighted, color-blind, auditorily biased, who has read the books that I have read. He should also be about my age.
Anthony Burgess

Every successful creative person creates with an audience of one in mind.
Kurt Vonnegut

Whenever I feel uneasy about my writing, I think: What would be the response of the people in the book if they read the book? That's my way of staying on track. Those are the people for whom I write.
Toni Morrison

When I write, I aim in my mind not toward New York but toward a vague spot a little to the east of Kansas. I think of the books on library shelves, without their jackets, years old, and a countryish teen-aged boy finding them, and having them speak to him. The reviews, the stacks in Brentano's, are just hurdles to get over, to place the books on that shelf.
John Updike

I write for myself and strangers. The strangers, dear Readers, are an afterthought.
Gertrude Stein

I don't think the artist should bother about his audience. His best audience is the person he sees in his shaving mirror every morning. I think that the audience an artist imagines, when he imagines that kind of thing, is a room filled with people wearing his own mask.
Vladimir Nabokov

There's only one person a writer should pay any attention to. It's not any damn critic. It's the reader.
William Styron

The whole duty of a writer is to please and satisfy himself, and the true writer always plays to an audience of one.
E.B. White

A man really writes for an audience of about ten persons. Of course, if others like it, that is clear gain. But if those ten are satisfied, he is content.
Alfred North Whitehead

Your audience is one single reader. I have found that sometimes it helps to pick out one person—a real person you know, or an imagined person and write to that one.
John Steinbeck

Ideally, the writer needs no audience other than the few who understand. It is immodest and greedy to want more.
Gore Vidal

The greatest part of a writer's time is spent in reading, in order to write; a man will turn over half a library to make one book.
Samuel Johnson

Reading is a consolation, if not always an inspiration. It lessens the pain of the gratuitousness of writing.
Darryl Pinckney

The great gift is the passion for reading. It is cheap, it consoles, it distracts, it excites, it gives you knowledge of the world and experience of a wide kind. It is moral illumination.
Elizabeth Hardwick

As in the sexual experience, there are never more than two persons present in the act of reading—the writer who is the impregnator, and the reader who is the respondent.
E.B. White

Magazines all too frequently lead to books and should be regarded by the prudent as the heavy petting of literature.
Fran Lebowitz

I never desire to converse with a man who has written more books than he has read.
Samuel Johnson

Easy reading is damned hard writing.
Nathaniel Hawthorne

You think your pain and your heartbreak are unprecedented in the history of the world, but then you read.
James Baldwin

People say that life is the thing, but I prefer reading.
Logan Pearsall Smith

BOOKS

A book ought to be an icepick to break up the frozen sea within us.
  Franz Kafka

Some books leave us free and some books make us free.
  Ralph Waldo Emerson

Books are . . . funny little portable pieces of thought.
  Susan Sontag

All books are either dreams or swords.
  Amy Lowell

Books rule the world, or at least those nations which have a written
language; the others do not matter.
  Voltaire

A book is not harmless simply because no one is consciously offended by it.
  T.S. Eliot

I have always come to life after coming to books.
  Jorge Luis Borges

I . . . am almost ashamed to own up, but once I opened books slowly,
with stately, plump imaginary orchestras going off in my head like
overtures, like music behind the opening credits in films, humming the title
page, whistling the copyright, turning myself into producer and pit band,
usher and audience.
  Stanley Elkin

A successful book cannot afford to be more than ten percent new.
  Marshall McLuhan

The possession of a book becomes a substitute for reading it.
  Anthony Burgess

Books take their place according to their specific gravity as surely as
potatoes in a tub.
  Ralph Waldo Emerson

Books will speak plain when counselors blanch.
  Francis Bacon

No furniture is so charming as books.
Sydney Smith

Some books are undeservedly forgotten; none are undeservedly remembered.
W.H. Auden

Some books are to be tasted, others to be swallowed, and some few to be chewed and digested.
Francis Bacon

Books should to one of these four ends conduce,
For wisdom, piety, delight or use.
John Denham

As a writer, I hold uncut pages to be comment on an owner and an insult to an author. A book for me is something to be read, not kept under glass or in a safe. I want to dogear it, to underline it, to annotate it, and mark my favorite passages, and make my own index on the blank pages at the back.
John Mason Brown

The reason why so few good books are written is that so few people who can write know anything.
Walter Bagehot

The multitude of books is making us ignorant.
Voltaire

There are books of which the backs and covers are by far the best parts.
Charles Dickens

The covers of this book are too far apart.
Ambrose Bierce

Books without knowledge of life are useless.
Ben Jonson

Books, nowadays, are printed by people who do not understand them, sold by people who do not understand them, read and reviewed by people who do not understand them, and even written by people who do not understand them.
G.C. Lichtenberg

Until one has some kind of professional relationship with books, one does not discover how bad the majority of them are.
George Orwell

What can we see, read, acquire but ourselves? Take the book, my friend, and read your eyes out, you will never find there what I find.
Ralph Waldo Emerson

We find little in a book but what we put there. But in great books, the mind finds room to put many things.
Joseph Joubert

I suggest that the only books that influence us are those for which we are ready, and which have gone a little farther down our particular path than we have yet got ourselves.
E.M. Forster

A book is a mirror: if an ass peers into it, you can't expect an apostle to look out.
G.C. Lichtenberg

A book is good company. It is full of conversation without loquacity. It comes to your longing with full instruction, but pursues you never.
Henry Ward Beecher

Never read any book that is not a year old.
Ralph Waldo Emerson

Never lend books, for no one ever returns them; the only books I have in my library are books that other folk have lent me.
Anatole France

Hard-covered books break up friendships. You loan a hard-covered book to a friend and when he doesn't return it you get mad at him. It makes you mean and petty. But twenty-five cent books are different.
John Steinbeck

What a sense of security in an old book which Time has criticized for us!
James Russell Lowell

Books that have now become classics—books that have had their day and now get more praise than perusal—always remind me of retired colonels and majors and captains who, having reached the age limit, find themselves retired on half pay.
Thomas Bailey Aldrich

A classic is something that everybody wants to have read and nobody wants to read.
Mark Twain

The oldest books are still only just out to those who have not read them.
Samuel Butler

No man understands a deep book until he has seen and lived at least part of its contents.
Ezra Pound

Books are good enough in their own way, but they are a mighty bloodless substitute for life.
Robert Louis Stevenson

Books succeed,
And lives fail.
Elizabeth Barrett Browning

A good book is the precious life-blood of a master spirit, embalmed and treasured up on purpose to a life beyond life.
John Milton

Books think for me.
Charles Lamb

When one can read, can penetrate the enchanted realm of books, why write?
Colette

The road to ignorance is paved with good editions.
George Bernard Shaw

A book on cheap paper does not convince. It is not prized, it is like a wheezy doctor with pigtail tobacco breath, who needs a manicure.
Elbert Hubbard

A man's library is a sort of harem, and tender readers have a great prudency in showing their books to a stranger.
Ralph Waldo Emerson

There is no such thing as a moral or an immoral book. Books are well written, or badly written. That is all.
Oscar Wilde

A book is made better by good readers and clearer by good opponents.
Friedrich Wilhelm Nietzsche

A bad book is as much a labor to write as a good one; it comes as sincerely from the author's soul.
Aldous Huxley

Every book is a failure.
George Orwell

A great book should leave you with many experiences, and slightly exhausted at the end.
William Styron

Books are the carriers of civilization. Without books, history is silent, literature dumb, science crippled, thought and speculation at a standstill. Without books, the development of civilization would have been impossible. They are engines of change, windows on the world, "lighthouses" (as a poet said) "erected in the sea of time." They are companions, teachers, magicians, bankers of the treasures of the mind. Books are humanity in print.
Barbara Tuchman

Americans like fat books and thin women.
Russell Baker

GENRES

Fantasy is literature for teenagers.
   Brian Aldiss

All the historical books which contain no lies are extremely tedious.
   Anatole France

What makes a good writer of history is a guy who is suspicious. Suspicion marks the real difference between the man who wants to write honest history and the one who'd rather write a good story.
   Jim Bishop

There's great scope in the historical novel, so long as it isn't by Mary Renault or Georgette Heyer.
   Anthony Burgess

Historical fiction is not only a respectable literary form; it is a standing reminder of the fact that history is about human beings.
   Helen M. Cam

A historical romance is the only kind of book where chastity really counts.
   Barbara Cartland

The essay is a literary device for saying almost everything about almost anything.
   Aldous Huxley

Among all kinds of writing, there is none in which authors are more apt to miscarry than in works of humor, as there is none in which they are more ambitious to excel.
   Joseph Addison

There are several kinds of stories, but only one difficult kind—the humorous.
   Mark Twain

Satire is moral outrage transformed into comic art.
   Philip Roth

The finest satire is that in which ridicule is combined with so little malice and so much conviction that it even rouses laughter in those who are hit.
   G.C. Lichtenberg

Satire is always as sterile as it is shameful and as impotent as it is insolent.
  Oscar Wilde

Satire concerns itself with logically extending a premise to its totally insane conclusion, thus forcing onto an audience a certain unwelcome awareness.
  Jules Feiffer

Satire is something that most American editors seem to be afraid of. I think the reason is that very few people penetrate it. Nine times out of ten it is taken quite seriously.
  H.L. Mencken

Satire is what closes on Saturday night.
  George S. Kaufman

Satires which the censor can understand are justly forbidden.
  Karl Kraus

There exists an inverse correlation between the size of a ball and the quality of writing about the sport in which the ball is used. There are superb books about golf, very good books about baseball, not very many good books about football, few good books about basketball, and no good books on beachballs.
  George Plimpton

The beginner who submits a detective novel longer than 80,000 words is courting rejection.
  Howard Haycraft

Love interest nearly always weakens a mystery because it introduces a type of suspense that is antagonistic to the detective's struggle to solve a problem.
  Raymond Chandler

The thriller is an extension of the fairy tale. It is melodrama so embellished as to create the illusion that the story being told, however unlikely, could be true.
  Eric Ambler

My theory is that people who don't like detective stories are anarchists.
  Rex Stout

Frankly, I am not one of those college professors who coyly boasts of enjoying detective stories—they are too badly written for my taste and bore me to death.
  Vladimir Nabokov

At least half the mystery novels published violate the law that the solution, once revealed, must seem to be inevitable.
  Raymond Chandler

The mystery story is really two stories in one: the story of what happened and the story of what appeared to happen.
  Mary Roberts Rinehart

There certainly does seem a possibility that the detective story will come to an end, simply because the public will have learnt all the tricks.
Dorothy Sayers

The detective novel is the art for art's sake of yawning philistinism.
V.S. Pritchett

The detective himself should never turn out to be the culprit.
S.S. Van Dine

To accept a mediocre form and make something like literature out of it is in itself rather an accomplishment.
Raymond Chandler

A good science fiction story is a story with a human problem, and a human solution, which would not have happened without its science content.
Theodore Sturgeon

A good science fiction story usually deals with a society distinctly different from the one we are familiar with; a society that does not exist and has never existed; that is completely imaginary. That imaginary society has to be built up in detail without internal contradiction even while the plot is unfolding. The society can't be skimped; it should (at its best) be as interesting as the plot and catch just as strongly at the reader's attention.
Isaac Asimov

I . . . don't particularly care for science fiction. I read some Jules Verne in my youth, but I'm not very interested in other planets. I like them where they are, in the sky.
W.H. Auden

BIOGRAPHY AND AUTOBIOGRAPHY

Biography broadens the vision and allows us to live a thousand lives in one.
Elbert Hubbard

Biography is a scrofulous cottage industry, done mostly by academics who get grants and have a good time going all over the place interviewing. How seldom it is that one has ever heard of the person writing the biography.
Elizabeth Hardwick

A well-written life is almost as rare as a well-spent one.
Thomas Carlyle

Every great man nowadays has his disciples, and it is always Judas who writes the biography.
Oscar Wilde

If a life be delayed till interest and envy are at an end, we may hope for impartiality, but must expect little intelligence; for the incidents which give excellence to biography are of a volatile and evanescent kind, such as soon escape the memory.
Samuel Johnson

I have not much interest in anyone's personal history after the tenth year, not even my own. Whatever one was going to be was all prepared before that.
Katherine Anne Porter

In writing biography, fact and fiction shouldn't be mixed. And if they are, the fiction parts should be printed in red ink, the fact parts in black ink.
Catherine Drinker Bowen

Just how difficult it is to write biography can be reckoned by anybody who sits down and considers just how many people know the real truth about his or her love affairs.
Rebecca West

What pursuit is more elegant than that of collecting the ignominies of our nature and transfixing them for show, each on the bright pin of a polished phrase?
Logan Pearsall Smith

Biography is a region bounded on the north by history, on the south by fiction, on the east by obituary, and on the west by tedium.
  Philip Guedalla

Biography is to give a man some kind of shape after his death.
  Virginia Woolf

Nobody can write the life of a man but those who have eaten and drunk and lived in social intercourse with him.
  Samuel Johnson

When you read a biography, remember that the truth is never fit for publication.
  George Bernard Shaw

Biographies are but the clothes and buttons of the man—the biography of the man himself cannot be written.
  Mark Twain

Just as there is nothing between the admirable omelette and the intolerable, so with autobiography.
  Hilaire Belloc

Autobiography is now as common as adultery, and hardly less reprehensible.
  John Grigg

An autobiography is only a "sort of life"—it may contain less [sic] errors of fact than a biography, but it is of necessity more selective.
  Graham Greene

Autobiography is an obituary in serial form with the last installment missing.
  Quentin Crisp

Most autobiographies are written by corpses.
  S.N. Behrman

Autobiography is an unrivalled vehicle for telling the truth about other people.
  Philip Guedalla

To start writing about your life is, from one standpoint, to stop living it. You must avoid adventures today so as to make time for registering those of yesterday.
  Ned Rorem

Only when one has lost all curiosity about the future has one reached the age to write an autobiography.
  Evelyn Waugh

A poet's autobiography is his poetry. Anything else can only be a footnote.
  Yevgeny Yevtushenko

FICTION

Fiction is history without tables, graphs, dates, imports, edicts, evidence, laws; history without hiatus—intelligible, simple, smooth.
> *William Gass*

History is the recital of facts represented as true. Fable, on the other hand, is the recital of facts represented as fiction.
> *Voltaire*

Journalism allows its readers to witness history; fiction gives its readers an opportunity to live it.
> *John Hersey*

All fiction for me is a kind of magic and trickery—a confidence trick, trying to make people believe something is true that isn't.
> *Angus Wilson*

A wondrous dream, a fantasy incarnate, fiction completes us, mutilated beings burdened with the awful dichotomy of having only one life and the ability to desire a thousand.
> *Mario Vargas Llosa*

Fiction is like a spider's web, attached ever so slightly perhaps, but still attached to life at all four corners.
> *Virginia Woolf*

I am not interested in fiction. I want faithfulness.
> *Anaïs Nin*

Good fiction is made of that which is real, and reality is difficult to come by.
> *Ralph Ellison*

Some things can only be said in fiction, but that doesn't mean they aren't true.
> *Aaron Latham*

Fiction gives counsel. It connects the present with the past, and the visible with the invisible. It distributes the suffering. It says we must compose ourselves in our stories in order to exist. It says if we don't do it, someone else will do it for us.
> *E.L. Doctorow*

Fiction reveals truths that reality obscures.
  Jessamyn West

Truth may be stranger than fiction, but fiction is truer.
  Frederic Raphael

Why *shouldn't* truth be stranger than fiction? Fiction, after all, has to make sense.
  Mark Twain

The truth is, we've not really developed a fiction that can accommodate the full tumult, the zaniness and crazed quality of modern experience.
  Saul Bellow

Reporting the extreme things as if they were the average things will start you on the art of fiction.
  F. Scott Fitzgerald

The trouble with fiction is that it makes too much sense, whereas reality never makes sense.
  Aldous Huxley

To tell about a drunken muzhik's beating his wife is incomparably harder than to compose a whole tract about the "woman question."
  Ivan Sergeyevich Turgenev

All that non-fiction can do is answer questions. It's fiction's business to ask them.
  Richard Hughes

Any fiction should be a story. In any story there are three elements: persons, a situation, and the fact that in the end something has changed. If nothing has changed, it isn't a story.
  Malcolm Cowley

Stories ought to judge and interpret the world.
  Cynthia Ozick

The good end happily, the bad unhappily—that is what fiction means.
  Oscar Wilde

Fiction ... is a chance to rework the events of your life so that you give the illusion of being the intelligence at the center of it.
  Nora Ephron

Fiction is nothing less than the subtlest instrument for self-examination and self-display that mankind has invented yet. Psychology and X-rays bring up some portentous shadows, and demographics and stroboscopic photography do some fine breakdowns, but for the full *parfum* and effluvia of being human, for feathery ambiguity and rank facticity, for the air and iron, fire and spit of our daily mortal adventure there is nothing like fiction: it makes sociology look priggish, history problematical, the film media two-dimensional, and the *National Enquirer* as silly as last week's cereal box.
  John Updike

JOURNALISM

Journalism is literature in a hurry.
    Matthew Arnold

Journalism is the entertainment business.
    Frank Herbert

Journalism consists largely in saying "Lord Jones died" to people who never knew Lord Jones was alive.
    G.K. Chesterton

The difference between journalism and literature is that journalism is unreadable and literature is not read.
    Oscar Wilde

The distinction between literature and journalism is becoming blurred; but journalism gains as much as literature loses.
    W.R. Inge

Literature is the art of writing something that will be read twice; journalism what will be grasped at once.
    Cyril Connolly

Modern journalism justifies its own existence by the great Darwinian principle of the survival of the vulgarist.
    Oscar Wilde

The indispensable requirement for a good newspaper: as eager to tell a lie as the truth.
    Norman Mailer

Journalists write because they have nothing to say, and have something to say because they write.
    Karl Kraus

The art of newspaper paragraphing is to stroke a platitude until it purrs like an epigram.
    Don Marquis

Journalism is the ability to meet the challenge of filling space.
    Rebecca West

LITERATURE

Literature is the question minus the answer.
    Roland Barthes

Literature is an answer to the questions that society asks itself about itself, but this answer is almost always unexpected.
    Octavio Paz

All literature is gossip.
    Truman Capote

Remarks are not literature.
    Gertrude Stein

To turn events into ideas is the function of literature.
    George Santayana

The word, the expression, the image is the true function of literature. *Not* ideas.
    Vladimir Nabokov

Literature is news that *stays* news.
    Ezra Pound

Literature is the effort of man to indemnify himself for the wrongs of his condition.
    Ralph Waldo Emerson

Literature could be said to be a sort of disciplined technique for arousing certain emotions.
    Iris Murdoch

Literature is recognizable through its capacity to evoke more than it says.
    Anthony Burgess

A losing trade, I assure you, sir: literature is a drug.
    George Borrow

Our high respect for a well-read man is praise enough of literature.
    Ralph Waldo Emerson

Literature is printed nonsense.
    August Strindberg

Literature is the next best thing to God.
  Edna O'Brien

Literature is the art of writing something that will be read twice.
  Cyril Connolly

Literature is the human activity that takes the fullest and most precise account of variousness, possibility, complexity, and difficulty.
  Lionel Trilling

In the civilization of today it is undeniable that, over all the arts, literature dominates, serves beyond all.
  Walt Whitman

Literature is simply the appropriate use of language.
  Evelyn Waugh

Literature: proclaiming in front of everyone what one is careful to conceal from one's immediate circle.
  Jean Rostand

Works of art and literature are not an entertainment or a diversion to amuse our leisure, but the one serious and enduring achievement of mankind—the notches on the bank of an irrigation channel which record the height to which the water once rose.
  Gerald Brenan

When a book, any sort of book, reaches a certain intensity of artistic performance it becomes literature.
  Raymond Chandler

The existence of good bad literature—the fact that one can be amused or excited or even moved by a book that one's intellect simply refuses to take seriously—is a reminder that art is not the same thing as cerebration.
  George Orwell

A curious thing about written literature: It is about four thousand years old, but we have no way of knowing whether four thousand years constitutes senility or the maiden blush of youth.
  John Barth

What is so wonderful about great literature is that it transforms the man who reads it towards the condition of the man who wrote, and brings to birth in us also the creative impulse.
  E.M. Forster

Literature is, primarily, a chain of connections from the past to the present. It is not reinvented every morning, as some bad writers like to believe.
  Gore Vidal

Literature is an investment of genius which pays dividends to all subsequent times.
  John Burroughs

I think it can be tremendously refreshing if a creator of literature has something on his mind other than the history of literature so far. Literature should not disappear up its own asshole, so to speak.
  Kurt Vonnegut

The literary sensibility is geared to the timeless, that is, to the now only as an avenue by which all time can be reached.
  John Simon

It takes a great deal of history to produce a little literature.
  Henry James

Literature is the orchestration of platitudes.
  Thornton Wilder

All of literature is a space in which a variety of writings, none of them original, blend and crash.
  Roland Barthes

Great Literature is simply language charged with meaning to the utmost possible degree.
  George Orwell

A great literature is chiefly the product of inquiring minds in revolt against the immovable certainties of the nation.
  H.L. Mencken

The chief difference between literature and life: In books, the proportion of exceptional to commonplace people is high; in reality, very low.
  Aldous Huxley

Literature always anticipates life. It does not copy it, but molds it to its purpose. The nineteenth century, as we know it, is largely an invention of Balzac.
  Oscar Wilde

Reality is not an inspiration for literature. At its best, literature is an inspiration for reality.
  Romain Gary

Medicine is my lawful wife. Literature is my mistress.
  Anton Chekhov

Literature—creative literature—unconcerned with sex, is inconceivable.
  Gertrude Stein

Literature is an occupation in which you have to keep proving your talent to people who have none.
  Jules Renard

The basic problem is that if God exists, what is the point of literature? And if He *doesn't* exist, what is the point of literature?
  Eugène Ionesco

The only sensible ends of literature are, first, the pleasurable toil of writing; second, the gratification of one's family and friends; and, lastly, the solid cash.
  Nathaniel Hawthorne

Literature flourishes best when it is half a trade and half an art.
   W.R. Inge

The land of literature is a fairy land to those who view it at a distance, but, like all other landscapes, the charm fades on a nearer approach, and the thorns and briars become visible.
   Washington Irving

No human being ever spoke of scenery for above two minutes at a time, which makes me suspect that we hear too much of it in literature.
   Robert Louis Stevenson

Literature thrives on taboos, just as all art thrives on technical difficulties.
   Anthony Burgess

While thought exists, words are alive and literature becomes an escape, not from, but into living.
   Cyril Connolly

The illusion of art is to make one believe that great literature is very close to life, but exactly the opposite is true. Life is amorphous, literature is formal.
   Françoise Sagan

One handles truths like dynamite. Literature is one vast hypocrisy, a giant deception, treachery. All writers have concealed more than they revealed.
   Anaïs Nin

In literature nothing that is not beautiful has any right to exist.
   William Butler Yeats

The greatest masterpiece in literature is only a dictionary out of order.
   Jean Cocteau

Masterpieces are no more than the shipwrecked flotsam of great minds.
   Marcel Proust

Today's literature: prescriptions written by patients.
   Karl Kraus

Only the more rugged mortals should attempt to keep up with current literature.
   George Ade

There is nothing like literature: I lose a cow, I write about her death, and my writing pays me enough to buy another cow.
   Jules Renard

In literature the ambition of a novice is to acquire the literary language; the struggle of the adept is to get rid of it.
   George Bernard Shaw

Literature is not a mere juggling of words; what matters is what is left unsaid, or what may be read between the lines.
   Jorge Luis Borges

To a large extent, contemporary literature is shaped by writing programs in universities. It's not that the writing programs harm people. But an awful lot of people influence people who shouldn't be influencing people ... Today the kids are standing on the shoulders of midgets.
    Stanley Elkin

Perversity is the muse of modern literature.
    Susan Sontag

Literature is mostly about sex and not much about having children and life is the other way 'round.
    David Lodge

The unusual is only found in a very small percentage, except in literary creations, and that is exactly what makes literature.
    Julio Cortázar

A species living under the threat of obliteration is bound to produce obliterature—and that's what we are producing.
    James Thurber

The literary world is made of little confederacies, each looking upon its own members as the lights of the universe; and considering all others as mere transient meteors, doomed soon to fall and be forgotten, while its own luminaries are to shine steadily on to immortality.
    Washington Irving

There is only one school of literature—that of talent.
    Vladimir Nabokov

In the beginning was the review copy, and a man received it from the publisher. Then he wrote a review. Then he wrote a book which the publisher accepted and sent on to someone else as a review copy. The man who received it did likewise. This is how modern literature came into being.
    Karl Kraus

Whenever I apply myself to writing, literature comes between us.
    Jules Renard

Literature, real literature, must not be gulped down like some potion which may be good for the heart or good for the brain—the brain, that stomach of the soul. Literature must be taken and broken into bits, pulled apart, squashed—then its lovely reek will be smelt in the hollow of the palm, it will be munched and rolled upon the tongue with relish; then, and only then, its rare flavor will be appreciated at its true worth and the broken and crushed parts will again come together in your mind and disclose the beauty of a unity to which you have contributed something of your own blood.
    Vladimir Nabokov

NOVELS AND
NOVELISTS

Novel, n. A short story padded.
  Ambrose Bierce

A novel is a mirror walking along a main road.
  Stendhal

A novel is never anything but a philosophy put into images.
  Albert Camus

A novel is an impression, not an argument.
  Thomas Hardy

The novel is rescued life.
  Hortense Calisher

A novel is a prose narrative of some length that has something wrong
with it.
  Randall Jarrell

The novel is an unknown man and I have to find him.
  Graham Greene

The novel is the highest example of subtle interrelatedness that man has
discovered.
  D.H. Lawrence

The novel is a game or joke shared between author and reader.
  Annie Dillard

The final test for a novel will be our affection for it, as it is the test of our
friends, and of anything else which we cannot define.
  E.M. Forster

All novels are experimental.
  Anthony Burgess

All novels are about minorities; the individual is a minority.
  Ralph Ellison

Novels are sweets.
  William Makepeace Thackeray

A good novel tells us the truth about its hero; but a bad novel tells us the truth about its author.
   G.K. Chesterton

When we want to understand grief beyond grief, or the eternal confrontation of man and woman, man and God, man and himself, we go to the novel.
   Richard Condon

To me a novel is something that's built around the character of time, the nature of time, and the effects that time has on events and characters. When I see a novel that's supposed to take place in twenty-four hours, I just wonder why the man padded out the short story.
   Frank O'Connor

The novel is practically a Protestant form of art; it is a product of the free mind, of the autonomous individual.
   George Orwell

Every novel worthy of the name is like another planet, whether large or small, which has its own laws just as it has its own flora and fauna.
   François Mauriac

I view the novel, a single novel as well as a writer's entire corpus, as a musical composition in which the characters are themes, from variation to variation completing an entire parabola; similarly for the themes themselves.
   Alberto Moravia

The novel is something that never was before and will not be again.
   Eudora Welty

Secrets. Need to disguise. The novel was born of this.
   Anaïs Nin

What is a novel but a universe in which action is endowed with form, where final words are pronounced, where people possess one another completely and where life assumes the aspect of destiny?
   Albert Camus

Human beings have their great chance in the novel.
   E.M. Forster

Reading about imaginary characters and their adventures is the greatest pleasure in the world. Or the second greatest.
   Anthony Burgess

Reading a novel is a deep and singular pleasure, a gripping and mysterious human activity that does not require any more moral or political justification than sex.
   Philip Roth

The love of novels is the preference of sentiment to the senses.
   Ralph Waldo Emerson

For the most part, our novel-reading is a passion for results.
Ralph Waldo Emerson

Reading novels—serious novels, anyhow—is an experience limited to a very small percentage of the so-called enlightened public. Increasingly, it's going to be a pursuit for those who seek unusual experiences, moral fetishists perhaps, people of heightened imagination, the troubled pursuers of the ambiguous self.
Jerzy Kosinski

Novels provide readers with something to read.
Philip Roth

It is the sexless novel that should be distinguished: the sex novel is now normal.
George Bernard Shaw

What is a novel but a peculiar and as yet unheard-of event? This is the proper meaning of this name; and much which in Germany passes as a novel is no novel at all, but a mere narrative, or whatever else you may like to call it.
Goethe

The American novel is a conquest of the frontier; as it describes experience it creates it.
Ralph Ellison

I'd rather win a water-fight in a swimming pool, or remain astride a horse that is trying to get out from under me, than write the great American novel.
Jack London

I miss the spirit of social activism in American literature of the '20s and '30s. In your novels I learn a lot about universities and teachers. They are well written, but they bore me.
Günter Grass

All modern American literature comes from one book by Mark Twain called *Huckleberry Finn.*
Ernest Hemingway

One should not be too severe on English novels; they are the only relaxation of the intellectually unemployed.
Oscar Wilde

A good novel is possible only after one has given up and let go.
Walker Percy

The real comic novel has to do with man's recognition of his unimportance in the universe.
Anthony Burgess

The serious novel is now almost in the same situation as poetry. Eventually the novel will simply be an academic exercise, written by academics to be used in classrooms in order to test the ingenuity of students.
Gore Vidal

A novel is a meditation on existence, seen through imaginary characters. The form is unlimited freedom. Throughout its history, the novel has never known how to take advantage of its endless possibilities.
   Milan Kundera

I did not begin to write novels until I had forgotten all I had learned at school and college.
   John Galsworthy

There are three rules for writing a novel. Unfortunately, no one knows what they are.
   W. Somerset Maugham

There are no laws for the novel. There never have been, nor can there be.
   Doris Lessing

Of course the novel is a mess; it always has been a mess.
   Walker Percy

One is improvising when one writes, and you pick up in the same way a musician starts to improvise and detect the inner structure of what he's playing—that's the way I think it works in the writing of a novel. You pick up the beat.
   Robert Stone

One ought to know a lot about reality before one writes realistic novels.
   John Barth

Life resembles a novel more often than novels resemble life.
   George Sand

It's important that a novel be approached with some urgency. Spend too long on it, or have great gaps between writing sessions, and the unity of the work tends to be lost.
   Anthony Burgess

I think a novel should follow the fortunes of more than one character.
   Philip Larkin

A novel has to limit itself to the crew of a ship or a family; it's not a great way to process a huge number of people.
   Kurt Vonnegut

The first thing you have to consider when writing a novel is your story, and then your story—and then your story!
   Ford Madox Ford

In any work that is truly creative, I believe, the writer cannot be omniscient in advance about the effects that he proposes to produce. The suspense of a novel is not only in the reader, but in the novelist, who is intensely curious about what will happen to the hero.
   Mary McCarthy

The human race needs the novel. We need all the experience we can get. Those who say the novel is dead can't write them.
   Bernard Malamud

I would sooner read a time-table or a catalogue than nothing at all . . .
They are much more entertaining than half the novels that are written.
  W. Somerset Maugham

To write a novel may be pure pleasure. To live a novel presents certain
difficulties. As for reading a novel, I do my best to get out of it.
  Karl Kraus

A novelist is a person who lives in other people's skins.
  E.L. Doctorow

A novelist is the only writer who can make a name without a style, which
is only one more reason for not bothering with the novel.
  Robert Frost

The novelist is a shaman who is . . . offering his experience for the use of
the rest of the tribe.
  Russell Hoban

The novelist is, above all, the historian of conscience.
  Frederic Raphael

The business of the novelist is not to chronicle great events but to make
small ones interesting.
  Arthur Schopenhauer

The complete novelist would come into the world with a catalog of qual-
ities something like this. He would own the concentration of a Trappist
monk, the organizational ability of a Prussian field marshal, the insight
into human relations of a Viennese psychiatrist, the discipline of a man
who prints the Lord's prayer on the head of a pin, the exquisite sense of
timing of an Olympic gymnast, and by the way, a natural instinct and
flair for exceptional use of language.
  Leon Uris

Just as the painter thinks with his brush and paints, the novelist thinks
with his story.
  W. Somerset Maugham

They can't yank a novelist like they can a pitcher. A novelist has to go the
full nine, even if it kills him.
  Ernest Hemingway

A novelist must preserve a child-like belief in the importance of things
which common sense considers of no great consequence.
  W. Somerset Maugham

The stage conjuror is perhaps the only other person permitted to play
havoc with the minds of his audience and not be resented.
  Len Deighton

Unfortunately, thrashing your young woman doesn't make her admire you
more as a novelist.
  William Cooper

I suppose I am a born novelist, for the things I imagine are more vital and vivid to me than the things I remember.
  Ellen Glasgow

It is a fact that few novelists enjoy the creative labour, though most enjoy thinking about the creative labour.
  Arnold Bennett

I am a man, and alive. . .For this reason I am a novelist. And being a novelist, I consider myself superior to the saint, the scientist, the philosopher, and the poet, who are all great masters of different bits of man alive, but never get the whole hog.
  D.H. Lawrence

There never was a good biography of a good novelist. There couldn't be. He is too many people, if he's any good.
  F. Scott Fitzgerald

As artists, women novelists are rot, but as providers they are oil wells—they gush.
  Dorothy Parker

Essential characteristic of the really great novelist: a Christ-like, all-embracing compassion.
  Arnold Bennett

Unlike God, the novelist does not start with nothing and make something of it. He starts with himself as nothing and makes something of the nothing with the things at hand.
  Walker Percy

Have you noticed that in the overwhelming majority of modern novels the only real, three-dimensional, fully developed—living, breathing, and fornicating—person is the author, that is to say, some unmistakable alter ego and mouthpiece of the novelist?
  John Simon

The novelist is dead in the man who has become aware of the triviality of human affairs.
  W. Somerset Maugham

Most writers are not quick-witted when they talk. Novelists, in particular, drag themselves around in society like gut-shot bears.
  Kurt Vonnegut

POETS AND
POETRY

The poet is like the prince of the clouds, who rides the tempest and scorns the archer. Exiled on the ground, amidst boos and insults, his giant's wings prevent his walking.
   Charles Baudelaire

That hour is blessed when we meet a poet. The poet is brother to the dervish. He has no country nor is he blessed with the things of the world; and while we, poor creatures that we are, are worrying about fame, about power, about riches, he stands on a basis of equality with the powerful of the earth and people bow down before him.
   Aleksandr Sergeyevich Pushkin

A taste for drawing rooms has spoiled more poets than ever did a taste for gutters.
   Thomas Beer

Poets have to dream, and dreaming in America is no cinch.
   Saul Bellow

A poet, any real poet, is simply an alchemist who transmutes his cynicism regarding human beings into an optimism regarding the moon, the stars, the heavens, and the flowers, to say nothing of Spring, love, and dogs.
   George Jean Nathan

A famous poet is a discoverer, rather than an inventor.
   Jorge Luis Borges

Modesty is a virtue not often found among poets, for almost every one of them thinks himself the greatest in the world.
   Cervantes

All poets pretend to write for immortality, but the whole tribe have no objection to present pay and present praise.
   Charles Caleb Colton

True poets should be chaste, I know,
But wherefore should their lines be so?
   Catullus

A poet is not an author, but the subject of a lyric, facing the world in the first person.
   Boris Pasternak

The poet is a liar who always speaks the truth.
   Jean Cocteau

Anyone may be an honorable man, and yet write verse badly.
   Molière

Turn pimp, flatterer, quack, lawyer, parson, be chaplain to an atheist, or stallion to an old woman, anything but a poet; for a poet is worse, more servile, timorous and fawning than any I have named.
   William Congreve

A poet is, before anything else, a person who is passionately in love with language.
   W.H. Auden

A poet, with the exception of mysterious water-fluent tea-drinking *Auden,* must be a highly-conscious technical expert.
   Cyril Connolly

True poets are the guardians of the state.
   Wentworth Dillon

To become a poet is to take the whole field of human knowledge and human desire for one's province. . . but this field can only be covered by continual inner abdications.
   Lawrence Durrell

A poet can survive anything but a misprint.
   Oscar Wilde

To a poet, silence is an acceptable response, even a flattering one.
   Colette

In the case of many poets, the most important thing for them to do . . . is to write as little as possible.
   T.S. Eliot

An unromantic poet is a self-contradiction, like the democratic aristocrat that reads the *Atlantic Monthly.*
   Robert Frost

The public has an unusual relation with the poet. It does not even know that he is there.
   Randall Jarrell

The poet is the rock of defense for human nature.
   William Wordsworth

Poets die in different ways: most of them do not die into the grave, but into business or criticism.
   Robert Frost

Poets have gotten so careless, it's a disgrace. You can't pick up a page.
All the words slide off.
  William Gass

Poets have to learn karate, these days.
  Yevgeny Yevtushenko

Buffoons and poets are near related
And willingly seek each other out.
  Goethe

Poets arguing about modern poetry: jackals snarling over a dried-up well.
  Cyril Connolly

Nine-tenths of English poetic literature is the result either of vulgar
careerism, or of a poet trying to keep his hand in. Most poets are dead by
their late twenties.
  Robert Graves

Poets are like baseball pitchers. Both have their moments. The intervals
are the tough things.
  Robert Frost

To be a poet is a condition rather than a profession.
  Robert Graves

A good poet's made as well as born.
  Ben Jonson

The true poet is a friendly man. He takes to his arms even cold and
inanimate things, and rejoices in his heart.
  Henry Wadsworth Longfellow

The best poets, after all, exhibit only a tame and civil side of nature. They
have not seen the west side of any mountain.
  Henry David Thoreau

Of all mankind the great poet is the equable man. Not in him but off from
him things are grotesque or eccentric or fail of their sanity.
  Walt Whitman

A great poet, a really great poet, is the most unpoetical of all creatures.
But inferior poets are absolutely fascinating.
  Oscar Wilde

Democritus maintains that there can be no great poet without a spice
of madness.
  Cicero

The man is either crazy or he is a poet.
  Horace

The courage of the poet is to keep ajar the door that leads into madness.
  Christopher Morley

Perhaps no person can be a poet, or can even enjoy poetry, without a certain unsoundness of mind.
Thomas Babington Macaulay

All poets are mad.
Robert Burton

It seems that God took away the minds of poets that they might better express His.
Socrates

The poet presents his thoughts festively, on the carriage of rhythm: usually because they could not walk.
Friedrich Wilhelm Nietzsche

No wonder poets sometimes have to *seem*
So much more business-like than business men.
Their wares are so much harder to get rid of.
Robert Frost

Poets were the first teachers of mankind.
Horace

Lyric poets generally come from homes run by women.
Milan Kundera

No honest poet can ever feel quite sure of the permanent value of what he has written: he may have wasted his time and messed up his life for nothing.
T.S. Eliot

Poets are born, not paid.
Wilson Mizner

The good poet sticks to his real loves, those within the realm of possibility. He never tries to hold hands with God or the human race.
Karl Shapiro

The bad poet is usually unconscious where he ought to be conscious, and conscious where he ought to be unconscious.
T.S. Eliot

I'd rather be a great bad poet than a good bad poet.
Ogden Nash

No bad man can be a good poet.
Boris Pasternak

All poets who, when reading from their own works, experience a choked feeling, are major. For that matter, all poets who read from their own works are major, whether they choke or not.
E.B. White

The poet is the unsatisfied child who dares to ask the difficult question which arises from the schoolmaster's answer to his simple question, and then the still more difficult question which arises from that.
Robert Graves

A poet more than thirty years old is simply an overgrown child.
H.L. Mencken

When one hears of a poet past thirty-five, he seems somehow unnatural and even a trifle obscene; it is as if one encountered a greying man who still played the Chopin waltzes and believed in elective affinities.
H.L. Mencken

Poets are almost always bald when they get to be about forty.
John Masefield

A poet should be treated with leniency and, even when damned, should be damned with respect.
Edgar Allan Poe

Poets are not to be seen.
Ralph Waldo Emerson

Sir, I admit your general rule,
That every poet is a fool;
But you yourself may serve to show it,
That every fool is not a poet.
Alexander Pope

Poets aren't very useful.
Because they aren't consumeful or very produceful.
Ogden Nash

The poet is a bird of strange moods. He descends from his lofty domain to tarry among us, singing; if we do not honor him he will unfold his wings and fly back to his dwelling place.
Kahlil Gibran

A poet is a nightingale who sits in darkness and sings to cheer its own solitude with sweet sounds.
Percy Bysshe Shelley

My quarrel with poets is not that they are unclear, but that they are too diligent.
E.B. White

No man can be explained by his personal history, least of all a poet.
Katherine Anne Porter

Poets are the unacknowledged legislators of the world.
Percy Bysshe Shelley

War talk by men who have been in a war is interesting, but moon talk by a poet who has not been in the moon is dull.
Mark Twain

Poets alone are permitted to tell the real truth.
Horace Walpole

The poet marries the language, and out of this marriage the poem is born.
W.H. Auden

Today's poet has less trouble making himself heard than making himself plain.
  Louis Untermeyer

A poet dares to be just so clear and no clearer; he approaches lucid ground warily, like a mariner who is determined not to scrape his bottom on anything solid. A poet's pleasure is to withhold a little of his meaning, to intensify by mistification. He unzips the veil from beauty, but does not remove it. A poet utterly clear is a trifle glaring.
  E.B. White

As a poet, there is only one political duty, and that is to defend one's language from corruption.
  W.H. Auden

The poet is he that hath fat enough, like bears and marmots, to suck his claws all winter.
  Henry David Thoreau

The poet is the priest of the invisible.
  Wallace Stevens

Poetry is what in a poem makes you laugh, cry, prickle, be silent, makes your toenails twinkle, makes you want to do this or that or nothing, makes you know that you are alone in the unknown world, that your bliss and suffering is forever shared and forever all your own.
  Dylan Thomas

Like a piece of ice on a hot stove the poem must ride on its own melting.
  Robert Frost

Information is true if it is accurate. A poem is true if it holds together.
  E.M. Forster

A poem is made up of thoughts, each of which filled the whole sky of the poet in its turn.
  Ralph Waldo Emerson

A poem begins in delight and ends in wisdom.
  Robert Frost

The poem is the dream made flesh, in a two-fold sense: as a work of art, and as life, which is a work of art.
  Henry Miller

Poetry is like fish: if it's fresh, it's good; if it's stale, it's bad; and if you're not certain, try it on the cat.
  Osbert Sitwell

Poetry isn't a kind of spray paint you use to cover selected objects with. A good poem about failure is a success.
  Philip Larkin

All bad poetry springs from genuine feeling.
  Oscar Wilde

I should define a good poem as one that makes complete sense; and says all it has to say memorably and economically, and has been written for no other than poetic reasons.
Robert Graves

A poem is good until one knows by whom it is.
Karl Kraus

A perfect poem is impossible. Once it had been written, the world would end.
Robert Graves

All good verses are like impromptus made at leisure.
Joseph Joubert

A good poem is a contribution to reality. The world is never the same once a good poem has been added to it. A good poem helps to change the shape and significance of the universe, helps to extend everyone's knowledge of himself and the world around him.
Dylan Thomas

All good poetry gives the illusion of a view of life.
T.S. Eliot

The best poem is that whose worked-upon unmagical passages come closest, in texture and intensity, to those moments of magical accident.
Dylan Thomas

It is easier to write a mediocre poem than to understand a good one.
Montaigne

The poem is not made from these letters that I drive in like nails, but of the white which remains on the paper.
Paul Claudel

The only really difficult thing about a poem is the critic's explanation of it.
Frank Moore Colby

When you read and understand a poem, comprehending its rich and formal meanings, then you master chaos a little.
Stephen Spender

Poetry is what gets lost in translation.
Robert Frost

In a poem the words should be as pleasing to the ear as the meaning is to the mind.
Marianne Moore

If it were not for poetry, few men would ever fall in love.
La Rochefoucauld

Love poems must be bounced back off a moon.
Robert Graves

Of our conflicts with others we make rhetoric; of our conflicts with ourselves we make poetry.
  William Butler Yeats

Poetry is more philosophical and of higher value than history.
  Aristotle

Too many people in the modern world view poetry as a luxury, not a
necessity, like petrol.
  John Betjeman

In poetry you have a form looking for a subject and a subject looking for
a form. When they come together successfully you have a poem.
  W.H. Auden

Perfect things in poetry do not seem strange, they seem inevitable.
  Jorge Luis Borges

A poem is the very image of life expressed in its eternal truth.
  Percy Bysshe Shelley

A poem should not mean, but be.
  Archibald MacLeish

The poem—that prolonged hesitation between sound and sense.
  Paul Valéry

Poetry is what Milton saw when he went blind.
  Don Marquis

Poetry is the deification of reality.
  Edith Sitwell

Poetry is the result of a struggle in the poet's mind between something he
wants to say and the medium in which he is trying to say it.
  Gerald Brenan

I know that poetry is indispensable, but to what I could not say.
  Jean Cocteau

If I feel physically as if the top of my head were taken off, I know that
is poetry.
  Emily Dickinson

Poetry is not an assertion of truth, but the making of that truth more fully
real to us.
  T.S. Eliot

Poetry is ordinary language raised to the nth degree.
  Paul Engle

Poetry's a mere drug, Sir.
  George Farquhar

True poetry makes things happen.
  Robert Graves

Poetry makes nothing happen: it survives
In the valley of its saying.
  W.H. Auden

Poetry is a mug's game.
  T.S. Eliot

Poetry is the impish attempt to paint the color of the wind.
  Maxwell Bodenheim

Not philosophy, after all, not humanity, just sheer joyous power of song,
is the primal thing in poetry.
  Max Beerbohm

Poetry is the synthesis of hyacinths and biscuits.
  Carl Sandburg

If a line of poetry strays into my memory, my skin bristles so that the
razor ceases to act.
  A.E. Housman

Poetry is the only art people haven't yet learned to consume like soup.
  W.H. Auden

Even when poetry has a meaning, as it usually has, it may be inadvisable
to draw it out ... Perfect understanding will sometimes always extinguish
pleasure.
  A.E. Housman

Poetry is trouble dunked in tears.
  Gwyn Thomas

Poetry is the bill and coo of sex.
  Elbert Hubbard

Poetry is life distilled.
  Gwendolyn Brooks

Poetry is the journal of a sea animal living on land, wanting to fly in
the air.
  Carl Sandburg

All poetry is putting the infinite with the finite.
  Robert Browning

Literature is a state of culture, poetry is a state of grace.
  Juan Ramón Jiménez

Poetry is the art of uniting pleasure with truth.
  Samuel Johnson

Boswell: Then, Sir, what is poetry?
Johnson: Why, Sir, it is much easier to say what it is not. We all *know*
what light is; but it is not easy to *tell* what it is.
  Boswell's Life of Johnson

Poetry is a report of some human experience ordered in terms of concepts involving a value judgment.
Joseph Wood Krutch

Two poetries are now competing, a cooked and a raw. The cooked, marvelously expert, often seems laboriously concocted to be tasted and digested by a graduate seminar. The raw, huge, blood-dripping gobbets of unseasoned experience are dished up for midnight listeners.
Robert Lowell

If poetry comes not as naturally as the leaves to a tree, it had better not come at all.
John Keats

I think that one possible definition of our modern culture is that it is one in which nine-tenths of our intellectuals can't read any poetry.
Randall Jarrell

Indifference to poetry is one of the most conspicuous characteristics of the human race.
Robert S. Lynd

If left to its own tendencies, I believe poetry would exclude everything but love and the moon.
Robert Frost

Poetry is the search for syllables to shoot at the barriers of the unknown and the unknowable.
Carl Sandburg

You will not find poetry anywhere unless you bring some of it with you.
Joseph Joubert

Poetry is the art of understanding what it is to be alive.
Archibald MacLeish

The crown of literature is poetry. It is its end aim. It is the sublimest activity of the human mind. It is the achievement of beauty and delicacy. The writer of prose can only step aside when the poet passes.
W. Somerset Maugham

To write good prose is an affair of good manners. It is, unlike verse, a civil art . . . Poetry is baroque.
W. Somerset Maugham

Poetry, surely, is a crisis, perhaps the only actionable one we can call our own.
J.D. Salinger

Poetry is all nouns and verbs.
Marianne Moore

Poetry . . . the mysteries of the irrational perceived through rational words.
Vladimir Nabokov

Poetry is language surprised in the act of changing into meaning.
  Stanley Kunitz

Poetry is the language in a state of crisis.
  Stephane Mallarmé

My verse represents a handle I can grasp in order not to yield to the centrifugal forces which are trying to throw me off the world.
  Ogden Nash

Poetry is the revelation of a feeling that the poet believes to be interior and personal which the reader recognizes as his own.
  Salvatore Quasimodo

Lying of an inspired, habitual, inventive kind, given a personality, a form, and a rhythm, is mainly what poetry is.
  James Dickey

Poetry should be great and unobtrusive, a thing which enters into one's soul, and does not startle it or amaze it with itself or with its subject.
  John Keats

I think poetry should surprise by a fine excess, but not by singularity; it should strike the reader as a wording of his own highest thoughts, and appear almost as a remembrance.
  John Keats

It is easier to think what poetry should be, than to write it.
  John Keats

Poetry is adolescence fermented, and thus preserved.
  José Ortega y Gasset

The blood jet is poetry
There is no stopping it.
  Sylvia Plath

Poetry is the renewal of words, setting them free, and that's what a poet is doing: loosening the words.
  Robert Frost

Poetry is fact given over to imagery.
  Rod McKuen

Poetry is a way of taking life by the throat.
  Robert Frost

Poetry is the rhythmical creation of beauty in words.
  Edgar Allan Poe

I have nothing to say and I am saying it and that is poetry.
  John Cage

A beautiful line of verse has twelve feet, and two wings.
  Jules Renard

I have no fancy ideas about poetry. It doesn't come to you on the wings of a dove. It's something you work hard at.
   Louise Bogan

If. . .it makes my whole body so cold no fire can warm me, I know that is poetry.
   Emily Dickinson

Poetry is a comforting piece of fiction set to more or less lascivious music.
   H.L. Mencken

Poetry is the presentment in musical form to the imagination, of noble grounds for the noble emotions.
   John Ruskin

I am overwhelmed by the beautiful disorder of poetry, the eternal virginity of words.
   Theodore Roethke

I've written some poetry I don't understand myself.
   Carl Sandburg

Poetry is a spot about half-way between where you listen and where you wonder what it was you heard.
   Carl Sandburg

Poetry is the silence and speech between a wet struggling root of a flower and sunlit blossom of that flower.
   Carl Sandburg

Poetry is the opening and closing of a door, leaving those who look through to guess about what was seen during a moment.
   Carl Sandburg

Poetry is what makes the invisible appear.
   Nathalie Sarraute

Poetry is a counterfeit creation, and makes things that are not, as though they were.
   John Donne

Poetry is a religion without hope.
   Jean Cocteau

Poetry is the spontaneous overflow of powerful feelings; it takes its origin from emotion recollected in tranquility.
   William Wordsworth

Poetry is the record of the best and happiest moments of the happiest and best minds.
   Percy Bysshe Shelley

Poetry is emotion put into measure. The emotion must come by nature, but the measure can be acquired by art.
   Thomas Hardy

Poetry and consumption are the most flattering of diseases.
William Shenstone

Great poetry is always written by somebody straining to go beyond what he can do.
Stephen Spender

Poetry is nothing less than the most perfect speech of man, that in which he comes nearest to being able to utter the truth.
Matthew Arnold

Poetry is the mathematics of writing and closely kin to music.
John Steinbeck

Ignorance is one of the sources of poetry.
Wallace Stevens

I could no more define poetry than a terrier can define a rat.
A.E. Housman

I like to think of poetry as statements made on the way to the grave.
Dylan Thomas

For me, poetry is an evasion of the real job of writing prose.
Sylvia Plath

Poetry makes its own pertinence, and a single stanza outweighs a book of prose.
Ralph Waldo Emerson

I wish our clever young poets would remember my homely definitions of prose and poetry; that is, prose—words in their best order; poetry—the best words in their best order.
Samuel Taylor Coleridge

Poetry is better understood in the verse of the artist than in the prose of the critic.
Matthew Arnold

Poetry is to prose as dancing is to walking.
John Wain

Poetry is simply the most beautiful, impressive, and widely effective mode of saying things.
Matthew Arnold

Poetry is mostly hunches.
John Ashbery

Poetry is the breath and finer spirit of all knowledge; it is the impassioned expression which is in the countenance of all Science.
William Wordsworth

Poetry provides the one permissible way of saying one thing and meaning another.
Robert Frost

Poems tell personal lies in order to express impersonal truths.
  Robert Pack

Poetry lies its way to the truth.
  John Ciardi

Blank verse, n. Unrhymed iambic pentameters—the most difficult kind of English verse to write acceptably; a kind, therefore, much affected by those who cannot acceptably write any kind.
  Ambrose Bierce

Free verse is like free love; it is a contradiction in terms.
  G.K. Chesterton

Writing free verse is like playing tennis with the net down.
  Robert Frost

No *vers* is *libre* for the man who wants to do a good job.
  T.S. Eliot

The writers of free verse got their idea from incorrect proof pages.
  Robert Frost

QUALIFICATIONS AND REQUIREMENTS

A writer needs three things, experience, observation and imagination, any two of which, at times any one of which, can supply the lack of the others.
William Faulkner

Unprovided with original learning, unformed in the habits of thinking, unskilled in the arts of composition, I resolved to write a book.
Edward Gibbon

The most essential gift for a good writer is a built-in shock-proof shit-detector.
Ernest Hemingway

To write fiction, one needs a whole series of inspirations about people in an actual environment, and then a whole lot of hard work on the basis of those inspirations.
Aldous Huxley

How can you write if you can't cry?
Ring Lardner

There is no need for the writer to eat a whole sheep to be able to tell what mutton tastes like. It is enough if he eats a cutlet.
W. Somerset Maugham

The longer I live the more I become convinced that the only thing that matters in literature is the (more or less irrational) *shamantsvo* of a book, i.e., that the good writer is first of all an enchanter.
Vladimir Nabokov

How vain it is to sit down to write when you have not stood up to live!
Henry David Thoreau

A writer doesn't need to go out and live, but stay home and invent.
Ned Rorem

How can you know that something is worth writing about if you haven't seen anything else?
Paul Theroux

It is necessary to remember and necessary to forget, but it is better for a writer to remember. It is necessary for him to live purposely, which is to say: to live and to remember having done so.
    William Saroyan

Real seriousness in regard to writing is one of the two absolute necessities. The other, unfortunately, is talent.
    Ernest Hemingway

To make a book is as much a trade as to make a clock; something more than intelligence is required to make an author.
    Jean de la Bruyère

An absolutely necessary part of a writer's equipment, almost as necessary as talent, is the ability to stand up under punishment, both the punishment the world hands out and the punishment he inflicts upon himself.
    Irwin Shaw

The essential condition to become a creator in the artistic domain, particularly in the novel, is to be able to enter into the skin of people.
    Georges Simenon

A writer who does not passionately believe in the perfectability of man has no dedication nor any membership in literature.
    John Steinbeck

A writer without a sense of justice and of injustice would be better off editing the Year Book of a school for exceptional children than writing novels.
    Ernest Hemingway

No one who cannot limit himself has ever been able to write.
    Nicolas Boileau

Context is all. And a relatively pure heart. *Relatively* pure—for if you had a pure heart you wouldn't be in the book-writing business in the first place.
    Robert Penn Warren

To be a writer you need to see things as they are, and to see things as they are you need a certain basic innocence.
    Tobias Wolff

A writer needn't know things in depth. If he speaks of something, he shouldn't know everything about it, only the things that go with his temperament. He should not be objective. One can discuss a subject in depth, but in a certain direction, not trying to cover the whole thing. For a writer the university is death.
    E.M. Cioran

The one absolute requirement for me to write . . . is to be awake.
    Isaac Asimov

Writing doesn't require drive. It's like saying a chicken has to have drive to lay an egg.
John Updike

All you need is a room without any particular interruptions.
John Dos Passos

I need noise and interruptions and irritation: irritation and discomfort are a great starter. The loneliness of doing it any other way would kill me.
Anita Brookner

The actual process of writing . . . demands complete, noiseless privacy, without even music; a baby howling two blocks away will drive me nuts.
William Styron

I like a room with a view, preferably a long view. I dislike looking out on gardens. I prefer looking at the sea, or ships, or anything which has a vista to it.
Norman Mailer

I prefer small messy rooms that don't look out on anything interesting.
William Maxwell

The ideal view for daily writing, hour on hour, is the blank brick wall of a cold-storage warehouse. Failing this, a stretch of sky will do, cloudless if possible.
Edna Ferber

A nice peaceful place with some good light.
Mary McCarthy

EGO

Every author, however modest, keeps a most outrageous vanity chained like a madman in the padded cell of his breast.
  Logan Pearsall Smith

My problem is intense vanity and narcissism. I've always had such a good physique and such intense charm that it's difficult to be true to myself.
  Lawrence Durrell

I am an enormously talented man, after all it's no use pretending that I am not and I was bound to succeed.
  Noel Coward

I've known all my life I could take a bunch of words and throw them up in the air and they would come down just right. I'm a semantic Paganini.
  Truman Capote

I'm the most translated writer in the world, behind Lenin, Tolstoy, Gorki and Jules Verne. And they're all dead.
  Mickey Spillane

No poet or novelist wishes he was the only one who ever lived, but most of them wish they were the only one alive, and quite a number fondly believe their wish has been granted.
  W.H. Auden

Writers become idiotic under flattery sooner than any other set of people in the world.
  Frank Moore Colby

Writers are too self-centered to be lonely.
  Richard Condon

Every writer thinks he is capable of anything. Scratch a Faulkner or a Hemingway and you'll find a man who thinks he can run the world.
  Norman Mailer

Writing a novel, especially a long novel, is an immense act of ego. You're not only asking people to pursue your vision, you're also asking them to pay to do so—and to applaud.
  William Gaddis

TALENT

Talent, and genius as well, is like a grain of pearl sand shifting about in the creative mind. A valued tormentor.
Truman Capote

Talent is like a faucet; while it is open, one must write. Inspiration is a farce that poets have invented to give themselves importance.
Jean Anouilh

What can any of us do with his talent but try to develop his vision, so that through frequent failures we may learn better what we have missed in the past.
William Carlos Williams

There is no substitute for talent. Industry and all the virtues are of no avail.
Aldous Huxley

Talent alone cannot make a writer. There must be a man behind the book.
Ralph Waldo Emerson

Any writer, I suppose, feels that the world into which he was born is nothing less than a conspiracy against the cultivation of his talent—which attitude certainly has a great deal to support it. On the other hand, it is only because the world looks on his talent with such a frightening indifference that the artist is compelled to make his talent important.
James Baldwin

I've put my genius into my life; I've only put my talent into my works.
Oscar Wilde

Everyone has talent. What is rare is the courage to follow the talent to the dark place where it leads.
Erica Jong

We do not write as we want but as we can.
W. Somerset Maugham

Talent is a matter of quantity: talent doesn't write one page, it writes three hundred.
Jules Renard

Having no talent is no longer enough.
Gore Vidal

ADVICE TO
YOUNG WRITERS

He that will write well in any tongue must follow this counsel of Aristotle: to speak as the common people do, to think as wise men do.
  Roger Ascham

Take care of the sense and the sounds will take care of themselves.
  Lewis Carroll

It is by sitting down to write every morning that one becomes a writer. Those who do not do this remain amateurs.
  Gerald Brenan

Be born anywhere, little embryo novelist, but do not be born under the shadow of a great creed, not under the burden of original sin, not under the doom of salvation.
  Pearl S. Buck

A writer shouldn't be engaged with other writers, or with people who make books, or even with people who read them. The farther away you get from the literary traffic, the closer you are to sources. I mean, a writer doesn't really *live*, he observes.
  Nelson Algren

A creative writer must study carefully the works of his rivals, including the Almighty.
  Vladimir Nabokov

There is only one place to write and that is *alone* at a typewriter. The writer who has to go *into* the streets is a writer who does not know the streets...*when you leave your typewriter you leave your machine gun and the rats come pouring through.*
  Charles Bukowski

For Godsake, keep your *eyes* open. Notice what's going on around you.
  William Burroughs

The most solid advice to a young writer is this, I think: try to learn to breathe deeply, really to taste food when you eat, and when you sleep, really to sleep. Try as much as possible to be wholly alive, with all your might, and when you laugh, laugh like hell, and when you get angry, get good and angry. Try to be alive. You will be dead soon enough.
  William Saroyan

Writing has laws of perspective, of light and shade, just as painting does, or music. If you are born knowing them, fine. If not, learn them. Then rearrange the rules to suit yourself.
    Truman Capote

It's not wise to violate the rules until you know how to observe them.
    T.S. Eliot

The discipline of the writer is to learn to be still and listen to what his subject has to tell him.
    Rachel Carson

You write a hit play the same way you write a flop.
    William Saroyan

To a chemist, nothing on earth is unclean. A writer must be as objective as a chemist; he must abandon the subjective line; he must know that dungheaps play a very respectable part in a landscape, and that evil passions are as inherent in life as good ones.
    Anton Chekov

Don't give up, because those who don't like your work may very well be wrong. And after you're published, don't pay any attention to the critics.
    Andrew Greeley

Never demean yourself by talking back to a critic, never. Write those letters to the editor in your head, but don't put them on paper.
    Truman Capote

Listen carefully to first criticisms of your work. Note just what it is about your work the critics don't like—then cultivate it. That's the part of your work that's individual and worth keeping.
    Jean Cocteau

I would recommend the cultivation of extreme indifference to both praise and blame because praise will lead you to vanity, and blame will lead you to self-pity, and both are bad for writers.
    John Berryman

For god's sake, don't do it unless you have to. . . It's not easy. It shouldn't be easy, but it shouldn't be impossible, and it's damn near impossible.
    Frank Conroy

If a young writer can refrain from writing, he shouldn't hesitate to do so.
    André Gide

The main suggestion from me is *read*. It is impossible for a writer to be able to write honestly and eloquently without having at one time or another acquainted himself with such writers as Sir Thomas Browne.
    William Styron

Read as many of the great books as you can before the age of 22.
    James Michener

Read, read, read. Read everything—trash, classics, good and bad, and see how they do it. Just like a carpenter who works as an apprentice and studies the master. Read! You'll absorb it. Then write. If it is good, you'll find out. If it's not, throw it out the window.
  William Faulkner

If you would be a reader, read; if a writer, write.
  Epictetus

Stop writing and start feeling.
  Lawrence Durrell

If you want to be true to life, start lying about it.
  John Fowles

Writing is easy; all you do is sit staring at a blank sheet of paper until the drops of blood form on your forehead.
  Gene Fowler

There's nothing to writing. All you do is sit down at a typewriter and open a vein.
  Red Smith

It's the writing that teaches you. It's the rotten stories that make it possible for you to write the good stories eventually.
  Isaac Asimov

Nothing you write, if you hope to be any good, will ever come out as you first hoped.
  Lillian Hellman

It helps to read the sentence aloud.
  Harry Kemelman

Never write about a place until you're away from it, because it gives you perspective. Immediately after you've seen something you can give a photographic description of it and make it accurate. That's good practice, but it isn't creative writing.
  Ernest Hemingway

The South understands language. You should live there if you want to be a writer.
  Rita Mae Brown

The last paragraph in which you tell what the story is about is almost always best left out.
  Irwin Shaw

Read over your compositions and, when you meet a passage which you think is particularly fine, strike it out.
  Samuel Johnson

Pay attention only to the form; emotion will come spontaneously to inhabit it. A perfect dwelling always finds an inhabitant.
  André Gide

Let your literary compositions be kept from the public eye for nine years at least.
   Horace

A little inaccuracy sometimes saves tons of explanation.
   Saki

One should never write down or up to people, but out of yourself.
   Christopher Isherwood

Write to please yourself. As you do, you'll reflect on your pages the thoughts and values of the people who share your own strange view of the world, and you'll remind them that they're not mad or alone.
   Richard Bach

Never write anything you think is "bestseller" material, because nobody really knows what makes a book a bestseller—and no good writer ever cares whether or not his book is a commercial success. What is important is always to do your best work.
   Gay Talese

Word-carpentry is like any other kind of carpentry: you must join your sentences smoothly.
   Anatole France

Only ambitious nonentities and hearty mediocrities exhibit their rough drafts. It is like passing around samples of one's sputum.
   Vladimir Nabokov

A good many young writers make the mistake of enclosing a stamped, self-addressed envelope, big enough for the manuscript to come back in. That is too much of a temptation to the editor.
   Ring Lardner

Be persistent. Editors change; editorial tastes change; markets change. Too many beginning writers give up too easily.
   John Jakes

Never submit an idea or chapter to an editor or publisher, no matter how much he would like you to . . . This is your story. Try and find out what your editor wants in advance, but then try and give it to him in one piece.
   John Creasey

It's not a good idea to try to put your wife into a novel. . . not your latest wife anyway.
   Norman Mailer

Writing is a wholetime job: no professional writer can afford only to write when he feels like it.
   W. Somerset Maugham

Get black on white.
   Guy de Maupassant

Sometimes you can lick an especially hard problem by facing it always the very first thing in the morning with the very freshest part of your mind. This has so often worked with me that I have an uncanny faith in it.
    F. Scott Fitzgerald

Oh, shun, lad, the life of an author.
    It's nothing but worry and waste.
Avoid that utensil,
The laboring pencil,
    And pick up the scissors and paste.
    Phyllis McGinley

Everyone who does not *need* to be a writer, who thinks he can do something else, ought to do something else.
    Georges Simenon

You must want to *enough*. Enough to take all the rejections, enough to pay the price in disappointment and discouragement while you are learning. Like any other artist you must learn your craft—then you can add all the genius you like.
    Phyllis Whitney

First of all, you must have an agent, and in order to get a good one, you must have sold a considerable amount of material. And in order to sell a considerable amount of material, you must have an agent. Well, you get the idea.
    Steve McNeil

Unless you think you can do better than Tolstoy, we don't need you.
    James Michener

No one put a gun to your head and ordered you to become a writer. One writes out of his own choice and must be prepared to take the rough spots along the road with a certain equanimity, though allowed some grinding of the teeth.
    Stanley Ellin

Nobody can advise and help you, nobody. There is only one single means. Go inside yourself. Discover the motive that bids you write; examine whether it sends its roots down to the deepest places of your heart, confess to yourself whether you would have to die if writing were denied you. This before all: ask yourself in the quietest hour of your night: *must* I write?
    Rainer Maria Rilke

Once you start illustrating virtue as such you had better stop writing fiction. Do something else, like Y-work. Or join a committee. Your business as a writer is not to illustrate virtue, but to show how a fellow may move toward it—or away from it.
    Robert Penn Warren

If you're going to write, don't pretend to write down. It's going to be the best you can do, and it's the fact that it's the best you can do that kills you!
    Dorothy Parker

Try to keep the rebel artist alive in you, no matter how attractive or exhausting the temptation.
   Norman Mailer

Lay off the muses, it's a very tough dollar.
   S.J. Perelman

The secret of popular writing is never to put more on a given page than the common reader can lap off it with no strain WHATSOEVER on his habitually slack attention.
   Ezra Pound

Get all the money you can in front and cash the check quickly.
   Larry L. King

Never make excuses, never let them see you bleed, and never get separated from your baggage.
   Wesley Price

My point to young writers is to socialize. Don't just go up to a pine cabin all alone and brood. You reach that stage soon enough anyway.
   Truman Capote

Better to write for yourself and have no public, than write for the public and have no self.
   Cyril Connolly

If you want to get rich from writing, write the sort of thing that's read by persons who move their lips when they're reading to themselves.
   Don Marquis

Keep going. Writing is finally play, and there's no reason why you should get paid for playing. If you're a real writer, you'll write no matter what.
   Irwin Shaw

Luxury is the wolf at the door and its fangs are the vanities and conceits germinated by success. When an artist learns this, he knows where the danger is.
   Tennessee Williams

You can't want to be a writer, you have to *be* one.
   Paul Theroux

In composing, as a general rule, run your pen through every other word you have written; you have no idea what vigor it will give to your style.
   Sydney Smith

When you catch an adjective, kill it.
   Mark Twain

Concision is honesty, honesty concision—that's one thing you need to know.
   John Simon

Write freely and as rapidly as possible and throw the whole thing on paper. Never correct or rewrite until the whole thing is down. Rewrite in process is usually found to be an excuse for not going on.
   John Steinbeck

Don't think and then write it down. Think on paper.
  Harry Kemelman

Advice to young writers who want to get ahead without any annoying delays: don't write about Man, write about a man.
  E.B. White

The idea is to get the pencil moving quickly.
  Bernard Malamud

To write quickly and to write well are usually incompatible attributes, and if you must choose one over the other, you should choose quality over speed every time.
  Isaac Asimov

Blot out, correct, insert, refine,
Enlarge, diminish, interline;
Be mindful, when invention fails,
To scratch your head, and bite your nails.
  Jonathan Swift

Not that the story need be long, but it will take a long while to make it short.
  Henry David Thoreau

If you are in difficulties with a book, try the element of surprise: attack it at an hour when it isn't expecting it.
  H.G. Wells

Avoid theatrical flourishes—the phrases that sound so damned good that they stand up and beg to be recognized as "good writing," and therefore must be struck from the text.
  Donald Spoto

With the pride of the artist, you must blow against the walls of every power that exists, the small trumpet of your defiance.
  Norman Mailer

A writer must refuse to allow himself to be transformed into an institution.
  Jean-Paul Sartre (on refusing the Nobel Prize)

Be obscure clearly.
  E.B. White

Authors—essayist, atheist, novelist,
  realist, rhymster, play your part,
Paint the mortal shame of nature
  with living hues of Art.
Rip your brothers' vices open, strip
  your own foul passions bare;
Down with Reticence, down with Reverence—
  forward—naked—let them stare.
  Alfred, Lord Tennyson

Write your heart out.
   Bernard Malamud

If the noun is good and the verb is strong, you almost never need an adjective.
   J. Anthony Lukas

As to the adjective: when in doubt, strike it out.
   Mark Twain

I think you can't learn to write, and people who spend money on writing courses would do much better to send the money to me, and I'll introduce them to an editor.
   Fran Lebowitz

Nice writing isn't enough. It isn't enough to have smooth and pretty language. You have to surprise the reader frequently, you can't just be nice all the time. Provoke the reader. Astonish the reader. Writing that has no surprises is as bland as oatmeal. Surprise the reader with the unexpected verb or adjective. Use one startling adjective per page.
   Anne Bernays

It's not enough just to have the ability, you have to want the life.
   Lawrence Block

If you can tell stories, create characters, devise incidents, and have sincerity and passion, it doesn't matter a damn how you write.
   W. Somerset Maugham

Be regular and orderly like a bourgeois, so that you may be violent and original in your work.
   Gustave Flaubert

I think a young poet, or an old poet, for that matter, should try to produce something that pleases himself personally, not only when he's written it but a couple of weeks later. Then he should see if it pleases anyone else, by sending it to the kind of magazine he likes reading. But if it doesn't, he shouldn't be discouraged.
   Philip Larkin

There is no advice to give young poets.
   Pablo Neruda

If I had to give young writers advice, I'd say don't listen to writers talking about writing or themselves.
   Lillian Hellman

MATERIAL

A writer's material is what he cares about.
  John Gardner

Every artist preserves deep within him a single source from which, throughout his lifetime, he draws what he is and what he says and when the source dries up the work withers and crumbles.
  Albert Camus

A writer uses what experience he or she has. It's the translating, though, that makes the difference.
  John Irving

A novelist is stuck with his youth. We spend it without paying much attention to how it will work out as material; nevertheless, we must draw on whatever was there for the rest of our lives. Our characters may grow old with us; we may invent or omit, fantasize or distort, their younger years, but we are all stuck.
  Vance Bourjaily

Most of the basic material a writer works with is acquired before the age of fifteen.
  Willa Cather

No one can ever write about anything that happened to him after he was twelve years old.
  Ignazio Silone

Almost all the great writers have as their *motif*, more or less disguised, the "passage from childhood to maturity," the clash between the thrill of expectation, and the disillusioning knowledge of the truth. *Lost Illusion* is the undisclosed title of every novel.
  André Maurois

Every writer has certain subjects that they write about again and again, and. . .most people's books are just variations on certain themes.
  Christopher Isherwood

I think one writes and rewrites the same book. I lead a character from book to book, I continue along with the same ideas. Only the angle of vision, the method, the lighting, change.
  Truman Capote

Mostly, we authors must repeat ourselves—that's the truth. We have two or three great moving experiences in our lives—experiences so great and moving that it doesn't seem at the time that anyone else has been caught up and pounded and dazzled and astonished and beaten and broken and rescued and illuminated and rewarded and humbled in just that way ever before.
F. Scott Fitzgerald

The work of every creator is autobiography, even if he does not know it or wish it, even if his work is "abstract." It is why you cannot re-do your work.
Jean Cocteau

The man who writes about himself and his own time is the only man who writes about all people and about all time.
George Bernard Shaw

In all my writing I tell the story of my life, over and over again.
Isaac Bashevis Singer

We're stuck with it in ourselves—what we can write about, if anything; what you can make articulate; what voices you have in your insides and in your ear.
Robert Penn Warren

And because I found I had nothing else to write about, I presented myself as a subject.
Montaigne

I am articulating as accurately as possible a graph of the activity of my conscience.
Allen Ginsberg

Almost every writer will tell you that events that happened to him before he starts writing are the most valuable to him. Once he starts writing he seems to observe the world through a filter.
Irwin Shaw

In literature, as in love, we are astonished at what is chosen by others.
André Maurois

Any writer is inevitably going to work with his own anxieties and desires. If the book is any good it has got to have in it the fire of a personal unconscious mind.
Iris Murdoch

I always use what remains of my dreams of the night before.
Eugène Ionesco

There are no dull subjects. There are only dull writers.
H.L. Mencken

Fundamentally, all writing is about the same thing: it's about dying, about the brief flicker of time we have here, and the frustrations that it creates.
Mordecai Richler

It's all right to learn things after you've written about them, but not too much ahead of time.
  John Barth

There should be no distinction between what we write down and what we really know.
  Allen Ginsberg

I've known a few men who were delighted at the possibility that I would write about them. "Have I been around long enough to make it into a short story?" one asked.
  Elizabeth Benedict

The opinions of an author are wrought by the superficial accidents of circumstance.
  Jorge Luis Borges

It's easier to write about those you hate—just as it's easier to criticize a bad play or a bad book.
  Dorothy Parker

I find it impossible to write about dumb people.
  Stanley Elkin

I didn't invent the world I write about—it's all true.
  Graham Greene

It is not a very fragrant world, but it is the world you live in, and certain writers with tough minds and a cool spirit of detachment can make very interesting and even amusing patterns out of it. It is not funny that a man should be killed, but it is sometimes funny that he should be killed for so little and that his death should be the coin of what we call civilization.
  Raymond Chandler

I'm at the service of the material that enters me. It takes me where it wants to go.
  Russell Hoban

While many things are too strange to be believed, nothing is too strange to have happened.
  Thomas Hardy

My writing is full of things seen, not heard. I get more material staring out at the world, not overhearing things.
  Ann Beattie

You can write about *anything*, and if you write well enough, even the reader with no intrinsic interest in the subject will become involved.
  Tracy Kidder

The void yields nothing. You have to be a great poet to make it ring.
  Jules Renard

Of all fatiguing, futile, empty trades, the worst, I suppose, is writing about writing.
  Hilaire Belloc

TOOLS

The tools I need for my work are paper, tobacco, food, and a little whiskey.
William Faulkner

I believe more in the scissors than I do in the pencil.
Truman Capote

I sort of curl up in a beat-up red easy chair and write, in longhand. I know it's old-fashioned, but at least I don't use a fountain pen any more. I used to, but I could never remember to fill it.
Louise Erdrich

I write in longhand. My Baltimore neighbor Anne Tyler and I are maybe the only two writers left who actually write with a fountain pen.
John Barth

Typewriter quotha!...I could never say what I would if I had to pick out my letters like a learned pig.
James Russell Lowell

The typewriter's my carpenter box.
Mickey Spillane

I believe that composing on the typewriter has probably done more than anything else to deteriorate English prose.
Edmund Wilson

The biggest obstacle to professional writing today is the necessity for changing a typewriter ribbon.
Robert Benchley

I know so little about the typewriter that once I bought a new one because I couldn't change the ribbon on the one I had.
Dorothy Parker

All I needed was a steady table and a typewriter . . . a marble-topped bedroom washstand table made a good place; the dining-room table between meals was also suitable.
Agatha Christie

The office equipment consists of one flat table, a sheaf of yellow paper and one of white. All the wheels, belts, wires, bolts, files, tools—the whole manufacturing process—has got to be contained in the space between my chin and my topmost hairpin.
  Edna Ferber

My schedule is flexible, but I am rather particular about my instruments: lined Bristol cards and well sharpened, not too hard, pencils capped with erasers.
  Vladimir Nabokov

Pencils must be round. A hexagonal pencil cuts my fingers after a long day.
  John Steinbeck

Up at school there's a typist who has one of those space-age typewriters, a word processor, and I can give her a story to type and once she has it typed and I get back the fair copy, I can mark it up to my heart's content and give it back to her; and the next day I can have my story back, all fair copy once more. Then I can mark it up again as much as I want, and the next day I'll have back a fair copy once more. I love it. It may seem like a small thing, really, but it's changed my life, that woman with her word processor.
  Raymond Carver

I work in longhand in a children's exercise book and then put it on a word processor.
  Dick Francis

The wastepaper basket is the writer's best friend.
  Isaac Bashevis Singer

IMAGINATION AND
INSPIRATION

Imagination, n. A warehouse of facts, with poet and liar in joint ownership.
>   *Ambrose Bierce*

Like a lot of what happens in novels, inspiration is a sort of spontaneous combustion—the oily rags of the head and heart.
>   *Stanley Elkin*

Divine fires do not blaze each day, but an artist functions in their afterglow, hoping for their recurrence.
>   *Ned Rorem*

Inspiration could be called inhaling the memory of an act never experienced.
>   *Ned Rorem*

I've always disliked words like *inspiration.* Writing is probably like a scientist thinking about some scientific problem, or an engineer about an engineering problem.
>   *Doris Lessing*

Inspiration comes out of the act of making an artifact, a work of craft.
>   *Anthony Burgess*

Invention . . . does not consist in creating out of void, but out of chaos.
>   *Mary Wollstonecraft Shelley*

One must still have chaos in oneself to be able to give birth to a dancing star.
>   *Friedrich Wilhelm Nietzsche*

Many characters have come to me. . . in a dream, and then I'll elaborate from there. I always write down all my dreams.
>   *William Burroughs*

You never have to change anything you got up in the middle of the night to write.
>   *Saul Bellow*

The best thoughts most often come in the morning after waking, while still in bed or during the walk.
>   *Leo Tolstoy*

Only those things are beautiful which are inspired by madness and written by reason.
  André Gide

Anyone who has ever been visited by the Muse is thenceforth haunted.
  T.S. Eliot

The devil himself always seems to get into my inkstand, and I can only exorcise him by pensful at a time.
  Nathaniel Hawthorne

Imagination grows by exercise and, contrary to common belief, is more powerful in the mature than in the young.
  W. Somerset Maugham

Having imagination, it takes you an hour to write a paragraph that, if you were unimaginative, would take you only a minute. Or you might not write the paragraph at all.
  Franklin P. Adams

I don't know why my imagination takes me where it does. I just feel so lucky to get a single idea for a novel that I can write about. When I get one, my ruminations and daydreaming grow and lead to other things, and I feel that there is a book there. I'm just so fortunate that I want to write it. I've never had more than one idea for a book at a time.
  Joseph Heller

Generalization is necessary to the advancement of knowledge; but particularity is indispensable to the creations of the imagination.
  Thomas Babington Macaulay

The imagination imitates. It is the critical spirit that creates.
  Oscar Wilde

What stimulates me to write a poem is that I have got something inside me that I want to get rid of—it is almost a kind of defecation.
  T.S. Eliot

If I get a promising idea I set it down, and it stays there. I don't make myself do anything with it.
  Marianne Moore

Our inventions mirror our secret wishes.
  Lawrence Durrell

I am a camera with its shutter open, quite passive, recording, not thinking.
  Christopher Isherwood

When they come, I write them; when they don't come, I don't.
  Jack Kerouac

I listen to the voices.
  William Faulkner

It is my heart that makes my songs, not I.
  Sara Teasdale

Heard melodies are sweet, but those unheard
Are sweeter.
John Keats

When I sit at my table to write, I never know what it's going to be till I'm under way. I trust in inspiration, which sometimes comes and sometimes doesn't. But I don't sit back waiting for it. I work *every* day.
Alberto Moravia

I don't wait to be struck by lightning and don't need certain slants of light in order to write.
Toni Morrison

Poetry is going on all the time inside, an underground stream. One can let down one's bucket and bring the poem back up.
John Ashbery

All you have to do is close your eyes and wait for the symbols.
Tennessee Williams

When I want to get going I read Faulkner. It's good because you can't write like him.
Ken Kesey

All there is is sitting down to work and trusting that the ignition key still turns everything on.
Peter Straub

I don't know anything about inspiration because I don't know what inspiration is; I've heard about it, but I never saw it.
William Faulkner

A writer is rarely so well inspired as when he talks about himself.
Anatole France

The unconscious mind has a habit of asserting itself in the afternoon.
Anthony Burgess

All writing comes by the grace of God.
Ralph Waldo Emerson

BEGINNINGS

I always begin with a character, or characters, and then try to think up as much action for them as possible.
John Irving

With me, a story usually begins with a single idea or memory or mental picture. The writing of the story is simply a matter of working up to that moment, to explain why it happened or what caused it to follow.
William Faulkner

Whether it's something that happened twenty years ago or only yesterday, I must start out with an emotion—one that's close to me and that I can understand.
F. Scott Fitzgerald

All my books literally come to me in the form of a sentence, an original sentence which contains the entire book.
Raymond Federman

I know very dimly when I start what's going to happen. I just have a very general idea, and then the thing develops as I write.
Aldous Huxley

I try to know as much as I can about a book before the beginning, but I never know exactly where it's going to end.
Scott Spencer

I have a pretty good sense of where the book is going to go. By temperament I am an incorrigible formalist, not inclined to embark on a project without knowing where I'm going.
John Barth

I've never outlined a novel before starting to write it—at the outset I've never been aware of the story I was trying to handle except in the most general terms. The beginnings of my novels have always been mere flickerings in the imagination, though in each case the flickerings have been generated, clearly enough, by a kind of emotional ferment that had been in process for some time.
John Hawkes

I don't see how anybody starts a novel without knowing how it's going to end. I usually make detailed outlines: how many chapters it will be and so forth.
John Barth

You cannot start a book with an intention, a calculation. You start writing before you know what you want to write or what it is you're doing.
E.L. Doctorow

I always start writing with a clean piece of paper and a dirty mind.
Patrick Dennis

You don't start with any aesthetic manifesto, you just do what works.
E.L. Doctorow

Beginning a book is unpleasant. I'm entirely uncertain about the character and the predicament, and a character in his predicament is what I have to begin with. Worse than not knowing your subject is not knowing how to treat it, because that's finally everything. I type out beginnings and they're awful, more of an unconscious parody of my previous book than the breakaway from it that I want. I need something driving down the center of a book, a magnet to draw everything to it—that's what I look for during the first months of writing something new.
Philip Roth

The beginning of a novel is a time of awful torment, when you're dealing with a lot of dead pieces and you have to wait and wait for some kind of animation.
Iris Murdoch

Before I start writing a novel I read *Candide* over again so that I may have in the back of my mind the touch-stone of that lucidity, grace and wit.
W. Somerset Maugham

I start at the beginning, go on to the end, then stop.
Anthony Burgess

I write the ending first. Nobody reads a book to get to the middle.
Mickey Spillane

You think about what actually happened, you tell friends long stories about it, you mull it over in your mind, you connect it together at leisure, then when the time comes to pay the rent again you force yourself to sit at the typewriter, or at the writing notebook, and get it over with as fast as you can.
Jack Kerouac

I always know the ending; that's where I start.
Toni Morrison

When I sit down to write a novel I do not at all know, and I do not very much care, how it is to end.
Henry James

I start with a tingle, a kind of feeling of the story I will write. Then come the characters, and they take over, they make the story.
  Isak Dinesen

Sometimes you get a line, a phrase, sometimes you're crying, or it's the curve of a chair that hurts you and you don't know why, or sometimes you just want to write a poem, and you don't know what it's about. I will fool around on the typewriter. It might take me ten pages of nothing, of terrible writing, and then I'll get a line, and I'll think, "That's what I mean!" What you're doing is hunting for what you mean, what you're trying to say. You don't know when you start.
  Anne Sexton

Mostly it's just a first line or an image or a vague sense of a situation.
  Bobbie Ann Mason

I usually spend a very long time thinking about it. Sometimes years. You know when you are able to write it. The work goes in before you start, really. You can have variations of the pattern, but the whole book must be there.
  Doris Lessing

I always have at the very start a curiously clear preview of the entire novel before me or above me.
  Vladimir Nabokov

I have never started a poem yet whose end I knew. Writing a poem is discovering.
  Robert Frost

When I write poetry, what I really get first is one or two phrases with a very insistent rhythm. The phrases keep insisting and the poem builds up by a process of accretion.
  Kenneth Rexroth

Usually the idea of a poem comes with a line or two of it, and they determine the rest.
  Philip Larkin

Usually I begin a poem with an image or phrase; if you follow trustfully, it's surprising how far an image can lead.
  James Merrill

If I didn't know the ending of a story, I wouldn't begin. I always write my last line, my last paragraphs, my last page first.
  Katherine Anne Porter

The last thing we decide in writing a book is what to put first.
  Blaise Pascal

ORIGINALITY

Originality is nothing but judicious imitation. The most original writers borrowed from one another. The instruction we find in books is like fire. We fetch it from our neighbors, kindle it at home, communicate it to others, and it becomes the property of all.
  Voltaire

What is originality? It is being one's self, and reporting accurately what we see and are.
  Ralph Waldo Emerson

Nothing is new except arrangement.
  Will Durant

Everything has been thought of before, but the problem is to think of it again.
  Goethe

Everything has been said before, but since nobody listens we have to keep going back and beginning all over again.
  André Gide

Who is original? Everything that we are doing, everything that we think, exists already, and we are only intermediaries, that's all, who make use of what is in the air.
  Henry Miller

About the most originality that any writer can hope to achieve honestly is to steal with good judgment.
  Josh Billings

A sequel is an admission that you've been reduced to imitating yourself.
  Don Marquis

Casting my mind's eye over the whole of fiction, the only absolutely original creation I can think of is *Don Quixote.*
  W. Somerset Maugham

An original writer is not one who imitates nobody, but one whom nobody can imitate.
  François-René de Chateaubriand

Derivative writers seem versatile because they imitate many others, past and present. Artistic originality has only itself to copy.
  Vladimir Nabokov

He has left off reading altogether to the great improvement of his originality.
  Charles Lamb

Originality does not consist in saying what no one has ever said before, but in saying exactly what you think yourself.
  J.F. Stephen

It is not permitted to a man, who takes up pen or chisel, to seek originality, for passion is his only business, and he cannot but mould or sing after a new passion because no disaster is like another.
  William Butler Yeats

The merit of originality is not novelty; it is sincerity. The believing man is the original man; whatsoever he believes, he believes it for himself, not for another.
  Thomas Carlyle

The original writer, as long as he isn't dead, is always scandalous.
  Simone de Beauvoir

Originality is undetected plagiarism.
  William Inge

If Thomas Wolfe sold, I'd write like Thomas Wolfe.
  Mickey Spillane

QUOTATION

Quoting: The act of repeating erroneously the words of another.
Ambrose Bierce

You could compile the worst book in the world entirely out of selected passages from the best writers in the world.
G.K. Chesterton

Classical quotation is the parole of literary men all over the world.
Samuel Johnson

When someone has the wit to coin a useful phrase, it ought to be acclaimed and broadcast or it will perish.
Jack Smith

Stay at home in your mind. Don't recite other people's opinions. I hate quotations. Tell me what you know.
Ralph Waldo Emerson

Pretty things that are well said—it's nice to have them in your head.
Robert Frost

To each reader those quotations are agreeable that neither strike him as hackneyed nor rebuke his ignorance.
H.W. Fowler

It is the little writer rather than the great writer who seems never to quote, and the reason is that he is never really doing anything else.
Havelock Ellis

The surest way to make a monkey of a man is to quote him.
Robert Benchley

I quote others only the better to express myself.
Montaigne

I often quote myself. It adds spice to my conversation.
George Bernard Shaw

Quotation confesses inferiority.
Ralph Waldo Emerson

Most anthologists. . . of quotations are like those who eat cherries. . . first picking the best ones and winding up by eating everything.
Nicolas Chamfort

By necessity, by proclivity, and by delight, we all quote.
Ralph Waldo Emerson

PLAGIARISM

Whatever has been well said by anyone is mine.
   Seneca

The difference between a bad artist and a good one is: The bad artist
seems to copy a great deal; the good one really does.
   William Blake

Great literature must spring from an upheaval in the author's soul. If that
upheaval is not present, then it must come from the works of any other
author which happen to be handy and easily adapted.
   Robert Benchley

Good swiping is an art in itself.
   Jules Feiffer

The Eighth Commandment was not made for bards.
   Samuel Taylor Coleridge

No man ever yet became great by imitation.
   Samuel Johnson

Immature artists imitate. Mature artists steal.
   Lionel Trilling

The immature poet imitates; the mature poet plagiarizes.
   T.S. Eliot

It has come to be practically a sort of rule in literature, that a man, having
once shown himself capable of original writing, is entitled thenceforth to
steal from the writings of others at discretion.
   Ralph Waldo Emerson

When a thing has been said and well said, have no scruple; take it and
copy it. Give references? Why should you? Either your readers know
where you have taken the passage and the precaution is needless, or they
do not know and you humiliate them.
   Anatole France

If we steal thoughts from the moderns, it will be cried down as plagiarism;
if from the ancients, it will be cried up as erudition.
   Charles Caleb Colton

Though old the thought and oft exprest,
'Tis his at last who says it best.
James Russell Lowell

Another illusion, seldom entertained by competent authors, is that the publisher's readers and others are waiting to plagiarize their work. I think it may be said that the more worthless the manuscript, the greater the fear of plagiarism.
Stanley Unwin

Plagiarists are always suspicious of being stolen from.
Samuel Taylor Coleridge

They lard their lean books with the fat of others' work.
Robert Burton

A plagiarist should be made to copy the author a hundred times.
Karl Kraus

When a man's talk is commonplace and his writings uncommon, it means that his talent lies in the place from which he borrows it, and not in himself.
Montaigne

Taking something from one man and making it worse is plagiarism.
George Moore

It is a mean thief, or a successful author, that plunders the dead.
Austin O'Malley

Every man is a borrower and a mimic, life is theatrical and literature a quotation.
Ralph Waldo Emerson

Steal! And egad, serve your best thoughts as gypsies do stolen children, disfigure them to make 'em pass for their own.
Richard Brinsley Sheridan

Adam was the only man who, when he said a good thing, knew that nobody had said it before him.
Mark Twain

Truth and reason are common to all and no more belong to him that spoke them heretofore than unto him that shall speak them hereafter.
Montaigne

When 'Omer smote 'is bloomin' lyre,
   He'd 'eard men sing by land and sea;
An' what 'e thought 'e might require,
   'E went an' took—the same as me!
Rudyard Kipling

I do borrow from other writers, *shamelessly!* I can only say in my defense, like the woman brought before the judge on a charge of kleptomania, "I do steal; but, Your Honor, only from the very best stores."
Thornton Wilder

I pinch.
Lawrence Durrell

WORK HABITS

It sounds shameful, but on my best days I write only about three or four hours.
Anne Bernays

I find that in the course of the day when I'm writing, after three or four hours of intense work, I have a splitting headache, and I have to stop.
Edward Albee

Thinking is the activity I love best, and writing to me is simply thinking through my fingers. I can write up to 18 hours a day. Typing 90 words a minute, I've done better than 50 pages a day. Nothing interferes with my concentration. You could put on an orgy in my office and I wouldn't look up—well, maybe once.
Isaac Asimov

I am a completely horizontal author. I can't think unless I'm lying down, either in bed or stretched on a couch and with a cigarette and coffee handy. I've got to be puffing and sipping. As the afternoon wears on, I shift from coffee to mint tea to sherry to martinis.
Truman Capote

I work mornings only. I go out to lunch. Afternoons I play with the baby, walk with my husband, or shovel mail.
Annie Dillard

The best regimen is to get up early, insult yourself a bit in the shaving mirror, and then pretend you're cutting wood.
Lawrence Durrell

A man may write at any time, if he will set himself doggedly to it.
Samuel Johnson

When my horse is running good, I don't stop to give him sugar.
William Faulkner

I write when I feel like it and wherever I feel like it, and I feel like it most of the time.
Jerzy Kosinski

I generally go to work right after breakfast. I sit right down to the machine. If I find I'm not able to write, I quit.
Henry Miller

After I get up it takes me an hour and a half of fiddling around before I can get up the courage and nerve to go to work. I smoke half a pack of cigarettes, drink six or seven cups of coffee, read over what I wrote the day before. Finally there's no further excuse. I go to the typewriter. Four to six hours of it. Then I quit and we go out. Or stay home and read.
James Jones

I prefer to get up very early in the morning and work. I don't want to speak to anybody or see anybody. Perfect silence. I work until the vein is out.
Katherine Anne Porter

The desk in the room, near the bed, with a good light, midnight till dawn, a drink when you get tired, preferably at home, but if you have no home, make a home out of your hotel room or motel room or pad: peace.
Jack Kerouac

I work every day—or at least I force myself into office or room. I may get nothing done, but you don't earn bonuses without putting in time. Nothing may come for three months, but you don't earn the fourth without it.
Mordecai Richler

I work every day, from ten in the morning till I'm done with my pages. I try not to write beyond a certain point. It's my experience that if I write too much in one day it kills a couple of days' work for me after that. I like to keep myself to three or four pages a day.
Scott Spencer

I start early in the morning. I'm usually out in the woods with the dog as soon as it gets light; then I drink a whole lot of tea and start as early as I can, and I go as long as I can.
Robert Stone

I always write in the morning. In the morning one's head is particularly fresh.
Leo Tolstoy

I work whenever I'm let.
Katherine Anne Porter

First coffee. Then a bowel movement. Then the muse joins me.
Gore Vidal

I find it easier to get up early in the morning, and I like to get through by one or two o'clock. I don't do very much in the afternoon. I like to get out of doors then if I can.
John Dos Passos

I spend the day at it, but that includes a lot of distractions.
Bobbie Ann Mason

You write by sitting down and writing. There's no particular time or place—you suit yourself, your nature. How one works, assuming he's disciplined, doesn't matter.
Bernard Malamud

I write whenever it suits me. During a creative period I write every day; a novel should not be interrupted. When I cease to be carried along, when I no longer feel as though I were taking down dictation, I stop.
   François Mauriac

My usual method. . . is to spend the mornings turning over the text in my mind. Then in the afternoon, between two and five, I call in a secretary and dictate to her. I can do about two thousand words. It took me about ten years to learn.
   James Thurber

I put a piece of paper under my pillow, and when I could not sleep I wrote in the dark.
   Henry David Thoreau

I never quite know when I'm not writing. Sometimes my wife comes up to me at a party and says, "Dammit, Thurber, stop writing." She usually catches me in the middle of a paragraph.
   James Thurber

I deemed it expedient to bind myself to certain self-imposed laws. It was also my practice to allow myself no mercy.
   Anthony Trollope

I do all my work before eleven in the morning. That's why I get up so early. Around five.
   May Sarton

I write every weekday morning.
   John Updike

I like to work in my bathrobe and pajamas, after breakfast, until I suddenly perceive, from what's on the page in the typewriter, that I've lost my judgment. And then I stop.
   William Maxwell

I like to stay up late at night and get drunk and sleep late. I wish I could break the habit but I can't. The afternoon is the only time I have left and I try to use it to the best advantage, with a hangover.
   William Styron

I need an hour alone before dinner, with a drink, to go over what I've done that day. I can't do it late in the afternoon because I'm too close to it. Also, the drink helps. It removes me from the pages.
   Joan Didion

There comes a moment in the day, when you have written your pages in the morning, attended to your correspondence in the afternoon, and have nothing further to do. Then comes the hour when you are bored; that's the time for sex.
   H.G. Wells

I get up in the morning, torture a typewriter until it screams, then stop.
   Clarence Budington Kelland

When I stop [working], the rest of the day is posthumous. I'm only really alive when I'm working.
   Tennessee Williams

DRINK

Many contemporary authors drink more than they write.
Maxim Gorky

Boozing does not necessarily have to go hand in hand with being a writer, as seems to be the concept in America. I therefore solemnly declare to all young men trying to become writers that they do not actually have to become drunkards first.
James Jones

Almost all American writers are alcoholic.
Gore Vidal

I don't drink a lot. That's perhaps one of the reasons why my characters are always drinking and taking drugs, because I am not.
Robert Stone

Drinking makes you loquacious, as we all know, and if what you've got for company is a piece of paper, then you're going to talk to it. Just try to enunciate, and try to make sense.
Madison Smartt Bell

I have never written a serious word in my life under the influence of alcohol.
William Styron

I cannot write intoxicated in any way.
Robert Stone

I usually need a can of beer to prime me.
Norman Mailer

A man's prose style is very responsive—even a glass of sherry shows in a sentence.
John Cheever

Port speaks the sentences of wisdom.
George Meredith

I never write when I'm drunk.
W.H. Auden

No one, ever, wrote anything as well even after one drink as he would have done without it.
   Ring Lardner

I've gone on the wagon, but my body doesn't believe it. It's waiting for that whiskey to get in there . . . to get me going. I never drink while I'm working, but after a few glasses, I get ideas that would never have occurred to me dead sober.
   Irwin Shaw

Faulkner was a big drinker, went on wild binges but he never wrote much while drunk. He and others drank to broaden their vision, their exaltation or despair, or to flee from the agony of the pure pain of creation.
   William Styron

When I have one martini, I feel bigger, wiser, taller. When I have a second, I feel superlative. When I have more, there's no holding me.
   William Faulkner

American writers drink a lot when they're "blocked" and drunkenness—being a kind of substitute for art—makes the block worse.
   Anthony Burgess

Some American writers who have known each other for years have never met in the daytime or when both were sober.
   James Thurber

Before I start to write, I always treat myself to a nice dry martini. Just one, to give me the courage to get started. After that, I am on my own.
   E.B. White

Alcohol is like love: the first kiss is magic, the second is intimate, the third is routine. After that you just take the girl's clothes off.
   Raymond Chandler

After a few ounces, the old tunes wake up, the grandeur of jingling anguish, the lick and shimmer of language, the heartbreak at the core of things. . . At a certain glow-level my brilliancies assured me I was an angel writing in Paradise.
   Donald Newlove

One of the disadvantages of wine is that it makes a man mistake words for thoughts.
   Samuel Johnson

I can't write without wine.
   Tennessee Williams

CHARACTERS

Action is character.
  F. Scott Fitzgerald

You can never know enough about your characters.
  W. Somerset Maugham

If a writer is true to his characters they will give him his plot. Observations must play second fiddle to integrity.
  Phyllis Bottome

I don't feel sympathetic toward some characters, unsympathetic toward others. I don't love some characters, feel contempt for others. They have attitudes; I don't.
  Don DeLillo

Begin with an individual and you find that you have created a type; begin with a type and you find that you have created—nothing.
  F. Scott Fitzgerald

Of course I base my characters partly on the people I know—one can't escape it—but fictional characters are oversimplified; they're much less complex than the people one knows.
  Aldous Huxley

I sometimes lose interest in the characters and get much more interested in the trees and animals.
  Toni Morrison

When I used to teach creative writing, I would tell the students to make their characters want something right away—even if it's only a glass of water. Characters paralyzed by the meaninglessness of modern life still have to drink water from time to time.
  Kurt Vonnegut

Each writer is born with a repertory company in his head and. . .as you get older, you become more skillful in casting them.
  Gore Vidal

I don't have a very clear idea of who the characters are until they start talking.
  Joan Didion

You can't blame a writer for what the characters say.
Truman Capote

All of my characters are looking for transcendence, whether they know it or not. The reason that they don't find it, and the *only* reason that they don't find it, is that *I* can't.
Robert Stone

As much as I can give of myself I give of myself. There's no reason why not. And when I have to hide something, I let the character speak.
Isaac Bashevis Singer

Many of the characters are fools and they are always playing tricks on me and treating me badly.
Jorge Luis Borges

That trite little whimsy about characters getting out of hand; it is as old as the quills. My characters are galley slaves.
Vladimir Nabokov

My characters exasperate me.
Anita Brookner

When the characters are really alive before their author, the latter does nothing but follow them in their action, in their words, in the situations which they suggest to him.
Luigi Pirandello

The legend that characters run away from their authors—taking up drugs, having sex operations, and becoming president—implies that the writer is a fool with no knowledge or mastery of his craft. The idea of authors running around helplessly behind their cretinous inventions is contemptible.
John Cheever

The characters have their own lives and their own logic, and you have to act accordingly.
Isaac Bashevis Singer

You put a character out there and you're in their power. You're in trouble if they're in yours.
Ann Beattie

Naming your characters Aristotle and Plato is not going to make their relationship interesting unless you make it so on the page.
Annie Dillard

To pass judgment on people or characters in a book is to make silhouettes of them.
Cesare Pavese

Fuck structure and grab your characters by the time balls.
Jack Kerouac

Madame Bovary, *c'est moi.*
Gustave Flaubert

WORDS

Words are loaded pistols.
    Jean-Paul Sartre

Words are the supreme objects. They are *minded* things.
    William Gass

Words are . . . awkward instruments and they will be laid aside eventually, probably sooner than we think.
    William Burroughs

Words, as is well known, are the great foes of reality.
    Joseph Conrad

Words are an albatross to a writer—heavy, hopeless, fateful things. One writes to make words mean something new.
    Joy Williams

A word is not the same with one writer as with another. One tears it from his guts. The other pulls it out of his overcoat pocket.
    Charles Péguy

Words have basic inalienable meanings, departure from which is either conscious metaphor or inexcusable vulgarity.
    Evelyn Waugh

The person who does not respect words and their proper relationships cannot have much respect for ideas—very possibly cannot have ideas at all.
    John Simon

Words are really a mask. They rarely express the true meaning; in fact they tend to hide it.
    Herman Hesse

Every word is like an unnecessary strain on silence and nothingness.
    Samuel Beckett

Words are weapons.
    George Santayana

The difference between the right word and the almost right word is the difference between lightning and the lightning bug.
    Mark Twain

For your born writer, nothing is so healing as the realization that he has come upon the right word.
   Catherine Drinker Bowen

Why shouldn't we quarrel about a word? What is the good of words if they aren't important enough to quarrel over? Why do we choose one word more than another if there isn't any difference between them?
   G.K. Chesterton

There is always one right word; use it, despite its foul or merely ludicrous associations.
   Dylan Thomas

You don't choose a word if you're a writer as a golf pro chooses a club with the *shot* in mind. You choose it with *yourself* in mind—*your* needs, *your* passions. It has to carry the green, yes, but it must also carry *you*.
   Archibald MacLeish

Words have weight, sound and appearance; it is only by considering these that you can write a sentence that is good to look at and good to listen to.
   W. Somerset Maugham

Our words must seem to be inevitable.
   William Butler Yeats

Words should be an intense pleasure to a writer just as leather should be to a shoemaker.
   Evelyn Waugh

How describe the delicate thing that happens when a brilliant insect alights on a flower? Words, with their weight, fall upon the picture like birds of prey.
   Jules Renard

Words are the small change of thought.
   Jules Renard

Writing is an affair of words rather than soul, impulse, "sincerity," or an instinct for the significant. If the words aren't there, nothing happens.
   Paul Fussell

There are too many words in prose, and they take up altogether too much room.
   Edwin Arlington Robinson

Words have taken a terrible beating.
   John Fowles

A writer lives in awe of words for they can be cruel or kind, and they can change their meanings right in front of you. They pick up flavors and odors like butter in a refrigerator.
   John Steinbeck

We are in love with the word. We are proud of it.
   Normal Mailer

Words are all we have.
   Samuel Beckett

GRAMMAR

Grammar is the grave of letters.
   Elbert Hubbard

It is well to remember that grammar is common speech formulated.
   W. Somerset Maugham

To grammar even kings bow.
   Molière

Usage is the only test. I prefer a phrase that is easy and unaffected to a phrase that is grammatical.
   W. Somerset Maugham

English usage is sometimes more than mere taste, judgment and education—sometimes it's sheer luck, like getting across a street.
   E.B. White

Any fool can make a rule and every fool will mind it.
   Henry David Thoreau

A writer who can't write in a grammerly manner better shut up shop.
   Artemus Ward

Why care for grammar as long as we are good?
   Artemus Ward

You can be a little ungrammatical if you come from the right part of the country.
   Robert Frost

Damn the subjunctive. It brings all our writers to shame.
   Mark Twain

The adjective is the banana peel of the parts of speech.
   Clifton Fadiman

Grammar is a piano I play by ear. All I know about grammar is its power.
   Joan Didion

Word has somehow got around that the split infinitive is always wrong. That is a piece with the outworn notion that it is always wrong to strike a lady.
   James Thurber

STYLE

Style is character. A good style cannot come from a bad, undisciplined character.
Norman Mailer

Style is knowing who you are, what you want to say, and not giving a damn.
Gore Vidal

Style is the physiognomy of the mind, and a safer index to character than the face.
Arthur Schopenhauer

Style is the hallmark of a temperament stamped upon the material at hand.
André Maurois

Style is effectiveness of assertion.
George Bernard Shaw

He who has nothing to assert has no style and can have none.
George Bernard Shaw

Proper words in proper places, make the true definition of a style.
Jonathan Swift

Style is everything and nothing. It is not that, as is commonly supposed, you get your content and soup it up with style; style is absolutely embedded in the way you perceive.
Martin Amis

One doesn't consider style, because style is.
Robert Stone

I have no leisure to think of style or of polish, or to select the best language, the best English—no time to shine as an authoress. I must just think aloud, so as not to keep the public waiting.
Isabel Burton

Style is the mind skating circles round itself as it moves forward.
Robert Frost

There is such an animal as a nonstylist, only they're not writers—they're typists.
Truman Capote

A good stylist should have narcissistic enjoyment as he works. He must be able to objectivize his work to such an extent that he catches himself feeling envious and has to jog his memory to find that he is himself the creator. In short, he must display that highest degree of objectivity which the world calls vanity.
  Karl Kraus

I've been called a stylist until I really could tear my hair out. And I simply don't believe in style. The style is you.
  Katherine Anne Porter

Style has no fixed laws; it is changed by the usage of the people, never the same for any length of time.
  Seneca

The language must be careful and must appear effortless. It must not sweat. It must suggest and be provocative at the same time.
  Toni Morrison

What is written without effort is in general read without pleasure.
  Samuel Johnson

As for style of writing, if one has anything to say, it drops from him simply and directly, as a stone falls to the ground.
  Henry David Thoreau

I am unlikely to trust a sentence that comes easily.
  William Gass

To write simply is as difficult as to be good.
  W. Somerset Maugham

A man who thinks much of his words as he writes them will generally leave behind him work that smells of oil.
  Anthony Trollope

You don't know what it is to stay a whole day with your head in your hands trying to squeeze your unfortunate brain so as to find a word . . . Ah! I certainly know the agonies of style.
  Gustave Flaubert

I never took the smallest pains with my style, have never thought about it, and do not know or want to know whether it is a style at all or whether it is not; as I believe and hope, just common, simple straightforwardness. I cannot conceive how any man can take thought for his style without loss to himself and his readers.
  Samuel Butler

You write with ease to show your breeding.
But easy writing's curst hard reading.
  Richard Brinsley Sheridan

All the fun's in how you say a thing.
  Robert Frost

An author arrives at a good style when his language performs what is required of it without shyness.
Cyril Connolly

Many intelligent people, when about to write books, force on their minds a certain notion about style, just as they screw up their faces when they sit for their portraits.
G.C. Lichtenberg

I see but one rule: *to be clear*. If I am not clear, all *my world* crumbles to nothing.
Stendhal

Altogether, the style of a writer is a faithful representative of his mind; therefore, if any man wish to write a clear style, let him be first clear in his thoughts; and if any man would write in a noble style, let him first possess a noble soul.
Goethe

A good style must, first of all, be clear. It must not be mean or above the dignity of the subject. It must be appropriate.
Aristotle

Clear prose indicates the absence of thought.
Marshall McLuhan

A good style should show no sign of effort. What is written should seem a happy accident.
W. Somerset Maugham

No style is good that is not fit to be spoken or read aloud with effect.
William Hazlitt

Every style that is not boring is a good one.
Voltaire

A strict and succinct style is that, where you can take away nothing without loss, and that loss to be manifest.
Ben Jonson

The editorial "we" has often been fatal to rising genius; though all the world knows that it is only a form of speech, very often employed by a single needy blockhead.
Thomas Babington Macaulay

Only presidents, editors and people with tapeworm have the right to use the editorial "we."
Mark Twain

The greatest possible mint of style is to make the words absolutely disappear into the thought.
Nathaniel Hawthorne

It takes less time to learn to write nobly than to learn to write lightly and straightforwardly.
Friedrich Wilhelm Nietzsche

We are surprised and delighted when we come upon a natural style, for instead of an author we find a man.
  Blaise Pascal

Literary people are forever judging the quality of the mind by the turn of expression.
  Frank Moore Colby

If the word *arse* is read in a sentence, no matter how beautiful the sentence, the reader will react only to that word.
  Jules Renard

I think of myself as a stylist, and stylists can become notoriously obsessed with the placing of a comma, the weight of a semicolon.
  Truman Capote

Anyone who can improve a sentence of mine by the omission or placing of a comma is looked upon as my dearest friend.
  George Moore

All morning I worked on the proof of one of my poems, and I took out a comma; in the afternoon I put it back.
  Oscar Wilde

This morning I deleted the hyphen from "hell-hound" and made it one word; this afternoon I redivided it and restored the hyphen.
  Edwin Arlington Robinson

With sixty staring me in the face, I have developed inflammation of the sentence structure and a definite hardening of the paragraphs.
  James Thurber

A change of style is a change of subject.
  Wallace Stevens

Style comes only after long, hard practice and writing.
  William Styron

I have decided many a stylistic problem first by head, then by heads or tails.
  Karl Kraus

In stating as fully as I could how things really were, it was often very difficult and I wrote awkwardly and the awkwardness is what they called my style. All mistakes and awkwardness are easy to see, and they called it style.
  Ernest Hemingway

A story can be wrecked by a faulty rhythm in a sentence—especially if it occurs toward the end—or a mistake in paragraphing, even punctuation.
  Truman Capote

I am well aware that an addiction to silk underwear does not necessarily imply that one's feet are dirty. None the less, style, like sheer silk, too often hides eczema.
  Albert Camus

I write as I walk because I want to get somewhere and I write as straight as I can, just as I walk as straight as I can, because that is the best way to get there.
  H.G. Wells

When I write after dark the shades of evening scatter their purple through my prose.
  Cyril Connolly

TECHNIQUE

Technique alone is never enough. You have to have passion. Technique alone is just an embroidered potholder.
Raymond Chandler

Through the study of technique—not canoeing or logging or slinging hash—one learns the best, most efficient ways of making characters come alive, learns to know the difference between emotion and sentimentality, learns to discern, in the planning stages, the difference between the better dramatic action and the worse. It is this kind of knowledge ... that leads to mastery. Mastery is not something that strikes in an instant, like a thunderbolt, but a gathering power that moves through time, like weather.
John Gardner

You lose energy and you gain technique.
Carlos Fuentes

The best technique is none at all.
Henry Miller

I don't know about method. The *what* is so much more important than how.
Ezra Pound

TITLES

A good title is the title of a successful book.
   Raymond Chandler

You'll find a title and it'll have a certain excitement for you; it will evoke the book, it will push you along. Eventually, you will use it up and you will have to choose another title. When you find the one that doesn't get used up, that's the title you go with.
   E.L. Doctorow

Titles distinguish the mediocre, embarrass the superior, and are disgraced by the inferior.
   George Bernard Shaw

I have never been a title man. I don't give a damn what it is called.
   John Steinbeck

There is only one rule I know on a title. It must sound like the author and not like some sure-fire product of the title factory.
   James M. Cain

The problem with titling is that the novel itself is the essence of what you're trying to do but the title is the essence of the essence. That's why most of them smell like bad perfume.
   Tom Robbins

The title comes last.
   Tennessee Williams

TALKING
ABOUT IT

The writer must write what he has to say, not speak it.
Ernest Hemingway

I have a superstition that if I talk about plot, it's like letting sand out of a hole in the bottom of a bag.
Shirley Hazzard

I've never discussed my writing with others much, but I don't believe it can do any harm. I don't think that there's any risk that ideas or materials will evaporate.
Aldous Huxley

Writers talk too much.
Lillian Hellman

Why do people always expect authors to answer questions? I am an author because I want to *ask* questions. If I had answers I'd be a politician.
Eugène Ionesco

It is hard enough to write books and stories without being asked to explain them as well.
Ernest Hemingway

I just think it's bad to talk about one's present work, for it spoils something at the root of the creative act. It discharges the tension.
Norman Mailer

More often than not the writer who talks about something he's working on talks it right out of existence.
William Maxwell

The author should keep his mouth shut when his work begins to speak.
Friedrich Wilhelm Nietzsche

Never talk about what you are going to do until after you have written it.
Mario Puzo

Don't tell anybody what your book is about and don't show it until it's finished. It's not that anybody will steal your idea but that all that energy that goes into the writing of your story will be dissipated.
David Wallechinsky

It's rather hard to be a good artist and also be able to explain intelligently what your art is about.
  John Ashbery

I don't like to talk about work-in-progress because if I do then it's on TV 10 weeks later, and it takes me two to three years to write a novel because I do so much rewriting.
  Sidney Sheldon

I don't care to talk about a novel I'm doing because if I communicate the magic spell, even in an abbreviated form, it loses its force for me. Once you have talked, the act of communication has been made.
  Angus Wilson

If the poem can be improved by its author's explanations, it never should have been published.
  Archibald MacLeish

I can't understand these chaps who go around American universities explaining how they write poems: it's like going round explaining how you sleep with your wife.
  Philip Larkin

I don't like questions of explication. What did I mean by this or that? I want the books to speak for themselves.
  Bernard Malamud

I really talk too much about my work and to anyone who will listen. If I would limit my talk to inventions and keep my big mouth shut about work, there would probably be a good deal more work done.
  John Steinbeck

If there is a category of human being for whom his work ought to speak for itself, it is the writer.
  Isaac Asimov

You lose it if you talk about it.
  Ernest Hemingway

I have never heard much that any writer has said about writing that didn't embarrass me, including the things I say about it.
  John Barth

Anything a novelist (or any other artist) says about his own work should be regarded with suspicion . . . as Christopher Isherwood (in effect) once remarked—no writer is aware of more than about two-thirds of what he is actually doing and saying.
  Kingsley Amis

You shouldn't pay very much attention to anything writers say. They don't know why they do what they do. They're like good tennis players or good painters, who are just full of nonsense, pompous and embarrassing, or merely mistaken, when they open their mouths.
  John Barth

ANGST

Suffering is the main condition of the artistic experience.
  Samuel Beckett

Fear ringed by doubt is my eternal moon.
  Malcolm Lowry

Loneliness is your companion for life. If you don't want to be lonely, you get into TV.
  William Styron

Every creator painfully experiences the chasm between his inner vision and its ultimate expression. The chasm is never completely bridged. We all have the conviction, perhaps illusory, that we have much more to say than appears on the paper.
  Isaac Bashevis Singer

I am profoundly uncertain about how to write. I know what I love or what I like, because it's a direct, passionate response. But when I write I'm very uncertain whether it's good enough. That is, of course, the writer's agony.
  Susan Sontag

I have cultivated my hysteria with joy and terror.
  Charles Baudelaire

The arrogance of poets is only a defense; doubt gnaws at the greatest among them; they need our testimony to escape despair.
  François Mauriac

I find writing very nervous work. I'm always in a dither when starting a novel—that's the worst time. It's like going to the dentist, because you do make a kind of appointment with yourself.
  Kingsley Amis

For the modern consciousness, the artist (replacing the saint) is the exemplary sufferer. And among artists, the writer, the man of words, is the person to whom we look to be able best to express his suffering.
  Susan Sontag

All art is a kind of confession, more or less oblique. All artists, if they are to survive, are forced, at last, to tell the whole story; to vomit the anguish up.
 James Baldwin

If I feel it, I feel it now and then, but I don't try to cherish it nor do I feel especially proud of it. It comes on me, let's say, as a headache or toothache might come, and I do my best to discourage it.
 Jorge Luis Borges

Writing is not a profession but a vocation of unhappiness. I don't think an artist can ever be happy.
 Georges Simenon

If artists and poets are unhappy, it is after all because happiness does not interest them.
 George Santayana

Writing is pretty crummy on the nerves.
 Paul Theroux

It's a nauseous process.
 Rebecca West

Let's face it, writing is hell.
 William Styron

Writing is so difficult that I often feel that writers, having had their hell on earth, will escape all punishment hereafter.
 Jessamyn West

I'm not happy when I'm writing, but I'm more unhappy when I'm not.
 Fannie Hurst

I like to do and can do many things better than I can write, but when I don't write, I feel like shit. I've got the talent and I feel that I'm wasting it.
 Ernest Hemingway

Who casts to write a living line, must sweat.
 Ben Jonson

Writing is the diametric opposite of having fun. All of life, as far as I'm concerned, is an excuse not to write. I just write when fear overtakes me. It causes paralytic terror. It's really scary just getting to the desk—we're talking now five hours. My mouth gets dry, my heart beats fast. I react psychologically the way other people react when the plane loses an engine.
 Fran Lebowitz

It's a very excruciating life facing that blank piece of paper every day and having to reach up somewhere into the clouds and bring something down out of them.
 Truman Capote

When you're writing, that's when you're lonely. I suppose that gets into the characters you're writing about. There are hours and hours of silence.
 Dick Francis

When the going is good a writer knows very little, if any, loneliness. When it is bad he believes he knows nothing else.
William Saroyan

I used to greet each morning spitting blood in the washbasin, having the night before gnashed the inside of my mouth while dreaming I had misplaced a comma in my writing of that day, throwing off the pattern of speech given to a character who lived two hundred years ago. Years later a dentist asked me if I had a history of mental illness, because the mentally ill often exhibit the advanced molar grindings I did.
Thomas Sanchez

You have to sink way down to a level of hopelessness and desperation to find the book that you can write.
Susan Sontag

You can lie to your wife or your boss, but you cannot lie to your typewriter. Sooner or later you must reveal your true self in your pages.
Leon Uris

Nobody but a writer knows how exhausting it is to write. Nobody except perhaps a writer's wife. She knows what hell he goes through and how little he is paid for his efforts. I can write only three or four hours a day. After that I'm emotionally worn out.
Tennessee Williams

When God hands you a gift, he also hands you a whip; and the whip is intended solely for self-flagellation.
Truman Capote

The malaise of writing—and it is of no consequence whether the writer is talented or otherwise—is that after a time a man writing arrives at a point outside human relationships, becomes, as it were, ahuman.
Frederick Exley

The good writing of any age has always been the product of *someone's* neurosis, and we'd have a mighty dull literature if all the writers that came along were a bunch of happy chuckleheads.
William Styron

I do not understand this chronic illness. I wish I had gone to law school.
Darryl Pinckney

WRITER'S BLOCK

I've never been big on the agony of writing. I see no evidence that Tolstoy suffered from writer's block.
James Michener

When I feel difficulty coming on, I switch to another book I'm writing. When I get back to the problem, my unconscious has solved it.
Isaac Asimov

When I have trouble writing, I step outside my studio into the garden and pull weeds until my mind clears—I find weeding to be the best therapy there is for writer's block.
Irving Stone

The successful writer listens to himself. You get a writer's block by being aware that you're putting it out there.
Frank Herbert

It has been said that writing comes more easily if you have something to say.
Sholem Asch

I don't get writing blocks except from the stationer, but I do feel so sickened by what I write that I don't want to go on.
Anthony Burgess

There is always a point in the writing of a piece when I sit in a room literally papered with false starts and cannot put one word after another and imagine that I have suffered a small stroke, leaving me apparently undamaged but actually aphasic.
Joan Didion

I went for years not finishing anything. Because, of course, when you finish something you can be judged . . . I had poems which were rewritten so many times I suspect it was just a way of avoiding sending them out.
Erica Jong

The professional guts a book through . . . in full knowledge that what he is doing is not very good. Not to work is to exhibit a failure of nerve, and a failure of nerve is the best definition I know for writer's block.
John Gregory Dunne

Every writer I know has trouble writing.
Joseph Heller

GOOD WRITING

Good writing is a kind of skating which carries off the performer where he would not go.
 Ralph Waldo Emerson

Good writing is supposed to evoke sensation in the reader—not the fact that it's raining, but the feel of being rained upon.
 E.L. Doctorow

Good writing is true writing. If a man is making a story up it will be true in proportion to the amount of knowledge of life that he has had and how conscientious he is; so that when he makes something up it is as it would truly be.
 Ernest Hemingway

The best writing is rewriting.
 E.B. White

All good writing is *swimming under water* and holding your breath.
 F. Scott Fitzgerald

There is no royal path to good writing; and such paths as exist do not lead through neat critical gardens, various as they are, but through the jungles of self, the world, and craft.
 Jessamyn West

The secret of good writing is to say an old thing a new way or to say a new thing an old way.
 Richard Harding Davis

It has been said that good prose should resemble the conversation of a well-bred man.
 W. Somerset Maugham

When writing is good, everything is symbolic, but symbolic writing is seldom good.
 Wright Morris

Good writing excites me, and makes life worth living.
 Harold Pinter

People do not deserve good writing, they are so pleased with bad.
 Ralph Waldo Emerson

OUTPUT

[I'm] a sausage machine, a perfect machine.
  Agatha Christie

I'm a bleeder. It's a good day when I get a page done.
  S.J. Perelman

I wrote much because I was paid little.
  Anthony Burgess

I have the conviction that excessive literary production is a social offense.
  George Eliot

Wearing down seven number two pencils is a good day's work.
  Ernest Hemingway

Three hours a day will produce as much as a man ought to write.
  Anthony Trollope

2000 words a day is very good going.
  Evelyn Waugh

If my doctor told me I had only six months to live, I wouldn't brood. I'd type a little faster.
  Isaac Asimov

Only a small minority of authors over-write themselves. Most of the good and the tolerable ones do not write enough.
  Arnold Bennett

Unlike Andy Rooney, who puts out a book every year, I at least have the courtesy to wait two years before I offer something new.
  Art Buchwald

I'm a commercial writer, not an "author." Margaret Mitchell was an author. She wrote one book.
  Mickey Spillane

Nine out of ten writers, I am sure, could write more. I think they should and, if they did, they would find their work improving even beyond their own, their agent's, and their editor's highest hopes.
  John Creasey

Anthony Trollope trained himself to turn out forty-nine pages of manuscript a week, seven pages a day, and he was so rigorous about keeping to that exact number of pages that if he finished a novel halfway through the last day, he'd write the title of a new book and "Chapter One" on the next page and go right on until he'd done his proper quota of seven pages.
   Malcolm Cowley

Looking back, I imagine I was always writing. Twaddle it was too. But better far write twaddle or anything, anything, than nothing at all.
   Katherine Mansfield

If you have one strong idea, you can't help repeating it and embroidering it. Sometimes I think that authors should write one book and then be put in a gas chamber.
   John P. Marquand

Some men only have one book in them; others, a library.
   Sydney Smith

I can't turn out slews of stuff each day. I wish I could. I seem to have some neurotic need to perfect each paragraph—each sentence, even—as I go along.
   William Styron

The less you write, the better it must be.
   Jules Renard

PROCESS

I write the big scenes first, that is, the scenes that carry the meaning of the book, the emotional experience.
  Joyce Cary

The pattern of the thing precedes the thing. I fill in the gaps of the crossword at any spot I happen to choose. These bits I write on index cards until the novel is done.
  Vladimir Nabokov

I write any sort of rubbish which will cover the main outlines of the story, then I can begin to see it.
  Frank O'Connor

I do not write and never have written to an arranged plot. The book is composed at once like a picture, and may start anywhere, in the middle or at the end. I may go from the end to the beginning in the same day, and then from the beginning to the middle.
  Joyce Cary

While I have an idea of where I'm going, I don't have an outline. I just know a lot of stuff's going to happen that I'm not aware of when I start.
  Peter Maas

As for my next book, I am going to hold myself from writing it till I have it impending in me: grown heavy in my mind like a ripe pear; pendant, gravid, asking to be cut or it will fall.
  Virginia Woolf

I write books in quite a short time, usually no more than two months, with long periods in between when I just think.
  Lawrence Block

I don't write easily or rapidly. My first draft usually has only a few elements worth keeping. I have to find what those are and build from them and throw out what doesn't work, or what simply is not alive.
  Susan Sontag

I write fairly rapidly if I get going, and don't change much, and have never been one for making outlines or taking out whole paragraphs or agonizing much. If a thing goes, it goes for me, and if it doesn't go, I eventually stop and get off.
  John Updike

I don't write drafts. I do page one many, many times and move on to page two. I pile up sheet after sheet, each in its final state, and at length I have a novel that doesn't—in my view—need any revision.
  Anthony Burgess

I do a lot of revising. Certain chapters six or seven times. Occasionally you can hit it right the first time. More often, you don't.
  John Dos Passos

In composition, I do *not* think second thoughts are best.
  Lord Byron

Revision is just as important as any other part of writing and must be done *con amore*.
  Evelyn Waugh

I have rewritten—often several times—every word I have ever published. My pencils outlast their erasers.
  Vladimir Nabokov

Crappy work I do twice, good work I do three times.
  Paul Fussell

Some poets actually say they don't revise, don't believe in revising. They say their originality suffers. I don't see that at all. The words that come first are anybody's, a froth of phrases, like the first words from a medium's mouth. You have to make them your own.
  James Merrill

I never reread what I've written. I'm far too afraid to feel ashamed of what I've done.
  Jorge Luis Borges

I never reread a text until I have finished the first draft. Otherwise it's too discouraging.
  Gore Vidal

My first draft is *it*. I start at chapter 1, page 1, and plod on to THE END.
  Dick Francis

The first draft of anything is shit.
  Ernest Hemingway

I work four hours a day and then usually early in the evening I read over what I've written during the day and I do a lot of changing and shifting around. See, I write in longhand and I do two versions of whatever I'm doing. I write first on yellow paper and then I write on white paper and then when I finally have it more or less settled the way I want, then I type it. When I'm typing it, that's when I do my final rewrite. I almost never change a word after that.
  Truman Capote

I'll write a very rough first draft of every chapter, then I will rewrite every chapter. I try to get it down in the first rewrite, but some chapters I can't get quite right the third time. There are some I go over and over and over again.
　　Robert Stone

I rise at first light and I start by rereading and editing everything I have written to the point I left off. That way I go through a book I'm writing several hundred times. Most writers slough off the toughest but most important part of their trade—editing their stuff, honing it and honing it until it gets an edge like a bullfighter's killing sword. One time my son Patrick brought me a story and asked me to edit it for him. I went over it carefully and changed one word. "But, Papa," he said, "you've only changed one word." I said: "If it's the right word, that's a lot."
　　Ernest Hemingway

It takes me six months to do a story. I think it out and then write it sentence by sentence—no first draft. I can't write five words but that I change seven.
　　Dorothy Parker

I always write a story in one sitting.
　　Katherine Anne Porter

What I do is try and write a slab of ten thousand words, and if it doesn't come off, I do it again.
　　Lawrence Durrell

Each story tells me how to write *it*, but not the one afterwards.
　　Eudora Welty

I write . . . in notebooks in pencil, trying to complete each stanza before going on to the next. Then when the poem is finished I type it out, and sometimes make small alterations.
　　Philip Larkin

I revise the manuscript till I can't read it any longer, then I get somebody to type it. Then I revise the typing. Then it's retyped again. Then there's a third typing, which is the final one. Nothing should then remain that offends the eye.
　　Robert Graves

I like the physical aspect of writing. I like to tear up a piece of paper and throw it down and put a new piece of paper in the typewriter. When I've decided to change something, I like to retype the whole page.
　　E.L. Doctorow

Some authors type their works, but I cannot do that. Writing is tied up with the hand, almost with a special nerve.
　　Graham Greene

I write longhand and I type and I rewrite on the typed pages.
　　Joseph Heller

I wrote in longhand at first, but I've lost it. I use two fingers on the typewriter.
Dorothy Parker

I type in one place, but I write all over the house.
Toni Morrison

The best time for planning a book is while you're doing the dishes.
Agatha Christie

I always work on two things at a time. When one goes flat, I turn to the other.
Stephen Birmingham

I work on one project at a time, until it's completed, whether it takes a month like some of my stories, or seven years like some of my novels. I've never been able to think about the next thing I'm going to write while I'm writing.
John Barth

I never think when I write; nobody can do two things at the same time and do them well.
Don Marquis

I like to write when I feel spiteful; it's like having a good sneeze.
D.H. Lawrence

I write preferably in a state of semidepression. There has to be something that's not right. When one is in a neutral mood, why write? Why declare things?
E.M. Cioran

I write slowly because I write badly. I have to rewrite everything many, many times just to achieve mediocrity.
William Gass

I write fast because I have not the brains to write slow.
Georges Simenon

I never "plan" a stanza. Words cluster like chromosomes, determining the procedure.
Marianne Moore

I've always believed in writing without a collaborator, because where two people are writing the same book, each believes he gets all the worries and only half the royalties.
Agatha Christie

I never can understand how two men can write a book together; to me that's like three people getting together to have a baby.
Evelyn Waugh

My method is to take the utmost trouble to find the right thing to say, and then to say it with the utmost levity.
George Bernard Shaw

I always do the first line well, but I have trouble doing the others.
    Molière

I talk out the lines as I write.
    Tennessee Williams

I have begun to get the habit of trying to write all day and walking up and down the room between the lines; instead of rushing along as I always have, before the intuitions wore off. It makes me feel like a professional for the first time and no longer at the mercy of periods of inspiration and drought.
    Delmore Schwartz

I always leave off the day before. As Thomas Mann advised, when the going is good, when you know exactly where you are and you are in a moment of exuberance, you stop. When I hook on the next morning, if the going was good I just go. I feel it emotionally, almost in the blood, the pulse, the excitement.
    Marguerite Young

The real writing process is simply sitting there and typing the same old lines over and over and over and over and sheet after sheet after sheet gets filled with the same shit.
    William Gass

I sit comfortably in an armchair, opposite my secretary. Luckily, although she's intelligent, she knows nothing about literature and can't judge whether what I write is good or worthless. I speak slowly . . . and she takes it down.
    Eugène Ionesco

It's like making a movie: All sorts of accidental things will happen after you've set up the cameras. So you get lucky. Something will happen at the edge of the set and perhaps you start to go with that; you get some footage of that. You come into it accidentally. You set the story in motion, and as you're watching this thing begin, all these opportunities will show up.
    Kurt Vonnegut

We work in our own darkness a great deal with little real knowledge of what we are doing.
    John Steinbeck

When I'm near the end of the book, I sleep in the same room with it. Somehow the book doesn't leave you when you're asleep right next to it.
    Joan Didion

I don't know exactly how it's done. I let it alone a good deal.
    Saul Bellow

I'm not sure I understand the process of writing.
    Elizabeth Hardwick

POSTPARTUM

Finishing a book is just like you took a child out in the yard and shot it.
  Truman Capote

For a dyed-in-the-wool author nothing is so dead as a book once it is written. . .she is rather like a cat whose kittens have grown up.
  Rumer Godden

When a book is done, he has his own life and you forget about him. He goes and lives alone; he takes an apartment.
  Oriana Fallaci

The book dies a real death for me when I write the last word. I have a little sorrow and then go on to a new book which is alive. The rows of my books on the shelf are to me like very well embalmed corpses. They are neither alive nor mine. I have no sorrow for them because I have forgotten them, forgotten in its truest sense.
  John Steinbeck

I usually have a sense of clinical fatigue after finishing a book.
  John Cheever

Writing every book is like a purge; at the end of it one is empty . . . like a dry shell on the beach, waiting for the tide to come in again.
  Daphne du Maurier

I truly do not care about a book once it is finished. Any money or fame that results has no connection with my feelings with the book.
  John Steinbeck

I don't keep any copy of my books around . . . They would embarrass me. When I finish writing my books, I kick them in the belly, and have done with them.
  Ludwig Bemelmans

I scarcely look with full satisfaction upon any; for they do not seem what they might have been. I often wish that I could have twenty years more, to take them down from the shelf one by one, and write them over.
  Washington Irving

PUBLISHERS AND PUBLISHING

There are men that will make you books and turn 'em loose into the world with as much dispatch as they would do a dish of fritters.
Cervantes

Most publishers are basically commercial-minded. They have no time for literary idealism.
Irving Wallace

The only people who can be excused for letting a bad book loose on the world are the poor devils who have to write for a living!
Molière

You write a book, you invest your imagination in it, and then you hand it over to a bunch of people who have no imagination and no understanding of their own enterprise.
Saul Bellow

In spite of good will, and frequently of true friendship, Author and Publisher are natural antagonists. Authors, as everybody knows, are difficult—they are unreliable, arrogant, and grasping. But publishers are impossible—grasping, arrogant, and unreliable. Many publishing tangles come from the fact that authors and publishers are far too much alike.
Jacques Barzun

It circulated for five years, through the halls of fifteen publishers, and finally ended up with Vanguard Press, which, as you can see, is rather deep into the alphabet.
Patrick Dennis on Auntie Mame

It is with publishers as with wives: one always wants somebody else's.
Norman Douglas

Every author pisses and moans about his publisher.
Roy Blount, Jr.

No author is a man of genius to his publisher.
Heinrich Heine

A publisher who writes is like a cow in a milk bar.
Arthur Koestler

Before publishers' blurbs were invented, authors had to make their reputations by writing.
Laurence J. Peter

It is not wise to solicit the opinions of publishers—they become proud if you do.
Gore Vidal

I could show you all society poisoned by this class of person—a class unknown to the ancients—who, not being able to find any honest occupation, be it manual labor or service, and unluckily knowing how to read and write, become the brokers of literature, live on our works, steal our manuscripts, falsify them, and sell them.
Voltaire

As repressed sadists are supposed to become policemen or butchers, so those with irrational fear of life become publishers.
Cyril Connolly

Publishers never tell writers anything. They're all crazy and they drive me crazy.
Anne Bernays

Publishers are demons, there's no doubt about it.
William James

As part of my research for *An Anthology of Authors' Atrocity Stories About Publishers*, I conducted a study (employing my usual controls) that showed the average shelf-life of a trade book to be somewhere between milk and yogurt. It is true that some books by Harold Robbins or any member of the Irving Wallace family last longer on the shelves, but they contain preservatives.
Calvin Trillin

Of course no writers ever forget their first acceptance. One fine day when I was seventeen I had my first, second and third, all in the same morning's mail. Oh, I'm here to tell you, dizzy with excitement is no mere phrase!
Truman Capote

Having a book published is one of the all-time most satisfying experiences. It can't be matched by 10,000 hours of appearing on television. There it is, that tidy little package that represents so much of yourself.
Andy Rooney

For several days after my first book was published I carried it about in my pocket, and took surreptitious peeps at it to make sure the ink had not faded.
James M. Barrie

On the day the young writer corrects his first proof sheet he is as proud as a schoolboy who has just gotten his first dose of the pox.
Charles Baudelaire

First publication is a pure, carnal leap into that dark which one dreams is life.
Hortense Calisher

Literature is like any other trade; you will never sell anything unless you go to the right shop.
George Bernard Shaw

Publication is the auction of the Mind of Man.
Emily Dickinson

I publish a piece in order to kill it, so that I won't have to fool around with it any longer.
William Gass

In a very real sense, the writer writes in order to teach himself, to understand himself, to satisfy himself; the publishing of his ideas, though it brings gratifications, is a curious anticlimax.
Alfred Kazin

During the final stages of publishing a paper or book, I always feel strongly repelled by my own writing . . . it appears increasingly hackneyed and banal and less worth publishing.
Konrad Lorenz

When I finish something I can't wait. I've been lonely with it so I publish it in *samizdat*. It's as though the piece has been published when someone who's capable of understanding it receives it. That's the true publication.
Phillip Lopate

A person who publishes a book willfully appears before the populace with his pants down . . . If it is a good book nothing can hurt him. If it is a bad book, nothing can help him.
Edna St. Vincent Millay

Publication is a self-invasion of privacy.
Marshall McLuhan

If you would be thrilled by watching the galloping advance of a major glacier, you'd be ecstatic watching changes in publishing.
John D. MacDonald

The rules seem to be these: if you have written a successful novel, everyone invites you to write short stories. If you have written some good short stories, everyone wants you to write a novel. But nobody wants anything until you have already proved yourself by being published somewhere else.
James Michener

Publishing is a very mysterious business. It is hard to predict what kind of sale or reception a book will have, and advertising seems to do very little good.
Thomas Wolfe

I think it is the most curious lack of judgment to publish before you are ready. If there are echoes of other people in your work, you're not ready. If anybody has to help you rewrite your story, you're not ready. A story should be a finished work before it is shown.
Katherine Anne Porter

I don't think it's a good idea for writers to think too much about the publishing world. I sense in a good many books, even in books by the best writers, an anxiety about how it will do in the marketplace. You can feel it on the page, a sort of sweat of calculation.
Elizabeth Hardwick

Manuscript: something submitted in haste and returned at leisure.
Oliver Herford

Having been unpopular in high school is not just cause for book publication.
Fran Lebowitz

A copy of verses kept in the cabinet, and only shown to a few friends, is like a virgin much sought after and admired; but when printed and published, is like a common whore, whom anybody may purchase for half-a-crown.
Jonathan Swift

If you do not write for publication, there is little point in writing at all.
George Bernard Shaw

The unpublished manuscript is like an unconfessed sin that festers in the soul, corrupting and contaminating it.
Antonio Machado

Nothing stinks like a pile of unpublished writing.
Sylvia Plath

The printing-press is either the greatest blessing or the greatest curse of modern times, one sometimes forgets which.
James M. Barrie

I wonder whether what we are publishing now is worth cutting down trees to make paper for the stuff.
Richard Brautigan

Publishing a volume of verse is like dropping a rose-petal down the Grand Canyon and waiting for the echo.
Don Marquis

EDITORS AND EDITING

My definition of a good editor is a man I think charming, who sends me large checks, praises my work, my physical beauty, and my sexual prowess, and who has a stranglehold on the publisher and the bank.
   John Cheever

A magazine editor is a man who lives on a sort of spiritual Bataan, with bombs of odium taking him incessantly from the front and torpedoes of obloquy harrying him astern.
   H.L. Mencken

An editor should have a pimp for a brother, so he'd have someone to look up to.
   Gene Fowler

Never buy an editor or publisher a lunch or a drink until he has bought an article, story or book from you. This rule is absolute and may be broken only at your peril.
   John Creasey

Editors know best what they want when they open up a manuscript and find it right there in front of them.
   Stanley Ellin

I usually have poor to absent relations with editors because they have a habit of desiring changes and I resist changes.
   William Gass

I think their job is to send checks. *They* think their job is rewriting. They should also praise you—every time you hand something in, they should say it's the best thing you've ever written. *And* send the check.
   Fran Lebowitz

No passion in the world is equal to the passion to alter someone else's draft.
   H.G. Wells

Every abridgement of a good book is a stupid abridgement.
   Montaigne

CRITICS AND CRITICISM

Critic, n. A person who boasts himself hard to please because nobody tries to please him.
  Ambrose Bierce

The first man who objected to the general nakedness and advised his fellows to put on clothes, was the first critic.
  Edwin L. Godkin

A critic is a man who expects miracles.
  James Gibbons Huneker

A critic is a gong at a railroad crossing clanging loudly and vainly as the train goes by.
  Christopher Morley

More people have been run off from reading more good books and good writers by the boring weighty smothering blatherings of lit-nit-pick academic dandies than by all other sources.
  Larry L. King

Drooling, driveling, doleful, depressing, dropsical drips.
  Sir Thomas Beecham

There be some men are born only to suck out the poison of books.
  Ben Jonson

These curious sucker fish who live with joyous vicariousness on other men's work and discipline with dreary words the thing which feeds them.
  John Steinbeck

A critic is a haunter of unquiet graves. He tries to evoke the presence of a living art, but usually succeeds only in disturbing the peace of the dead.
  M.J.C. Hodgart

Critics! Appalled I ventured on the name.
Those cutthroat bandits in the paths of fame.
  Robert Burns

A critic is a man created to praise greater men than himself, but he is never able to find them.
  Richard Le Gallienne

Insects sting, not in malice, but because they want to live. It is the same with critics; they desire our blood, not our pain.
Friedrich Wilhelm Nietzsche

Critics are like brushers of noblemen's clothes.
Francis Bacon

Critics are like pigs at the pastry cart.
John Updike

A critic is a necessary evil, and criticism is an evil necessity.
Carolyn Wells

Reviewers . . . actually newspaper persons who chat about books in the press . . . have been with us from the beginning and they will be with us at the end. They are interested in writers, not writing. In good morals, not good art. When they like something of mine, I grow suspicious and wonder.
Gore Vidal

The new race of academic reviewers may be cleverer, more conscientious, fairer than those who went before and they may take their job more seriously, but they are a complete disaster from everyone's point of view—publisher, book buyer, writer—because practically no one reads them. It is not just that they assume a higher dedication and a higher level of seriousness than exists among most intelligent, educated novel readers. They are quite simply too dull.
Auberon Waugh

Reviewers are not born but made, and they are made by editors.
Anthony Burgess

A book reviewer is usually a barker before the door of a publisher's circus.
Austin O'Malley

Reviewers, with some rare exceptions, are the most stupid and malignant race. As a bankrupt thief turns thief-taker in despair, so an unsuccessful author turns critic.
Percy Bysshe Shelly

Reviewers are usually people who would have been poets, historians, biographers, etc., if they could; they have tried their talents at one or at the other, and have failed; therefore they turn critics.
Samuel Taylor Coleridge

A man is a critic when he cannot be an artist, in the same way that a man becomes an informer when he cannot be a soldier.
Gustave Flaubert

A dramatic critic is a man who leaves no turn unstoned.
George Bernard Shaw

Has anybody ever seen a drama critic in the daytime? Of course not. They come out after dark, up to no good.
P.G. Wodehouse

A drama critic is a person who surprises the playwright by informing him of what he meant.
   Wilson Mizner

There is not a single dramatic critic in London who would deliberately set himself to misrepresent the work of any dramatist—unless, of course, he personally disliked the dramatist.
   Oscar Wilde

A true critic hath one quality in common with a harlot, never to change his title or his nature.
   Jonathan Swift

The trade of critic, in literature, music, and the drama, is the most degraded of all trades.
   Mark Twain

Many a critic seems more like a committee framing resolutions than a man writing down what he thinks.
   Frank Moore Colby

Each generation of critics does nothing but take the opposite of the truths accepted by their predecessors.
   Marcel Proust

The good critic is he who narrates the adventures of his soul among masterpieces.
   Anatole France

The test of a good critic is whether he knows when and how to believe on insufficient evidence.
   Samuel Butler

The only critics worth reading are the critics who practice, and practice well, the art of which they write.
   T.S. Eliot

A good critic is the sorcerer that makes some hidden spring gush forth unexpectedly under our feet.
   François Mauriac

Critics are probably more prone to clichés than fiction writers who pluck things out of the air.
   Penelope Gilliatt

As soon
Seek roses in December—ice in June;
Hope constancy in wind, or corn in chaff;
Believe a woman or an epitaph,
Or any other thing that's false, before
You trust in critics.
   Lord Byron

A man must serve his time at every trade save censure—critics all are ready made.
   Lord Byron

The artist is a cut above the critic, for the artist is writing something which will move the critic. The critic is writing something which will move everybody but the artist.
   William Faulkner

An artist is born kneeling; he fights to stand. A critic, by nature of the judgment seat, is born sitting.
   Hortense Calisher

They who are to be judges must also be performers.
   Aristotle

The world have paid too great a compliment to critics, and have imagined them men of much greater profundity than they really are.
   Henry Fielding

A good writer is not, *per se*, a good book critic. No more than a good drunk is automatically a good bartender.
   Jim Bishop

Those who write ill, and they who ne'er durst write,
Turn critics out of mere revenge and spite.
   John Dryden

Nature fits all her children with something to do,
He who would write and can't write, can surely review.
   James Russell Lowell

Every good poet includes a critic, but the reverse will not hold.
   William Shenstone

To literary critics a book is assumed to be guilty until it proves itself innocent.
   Nelson Algren

One battle doesn't make a campaign, but critics treat one book, good or bad, like a whole war.
   Ernest Hemingway

I'll give you fifty dollars if you produce a writer who can honestly say he was ever helped by the prissy carpings and condescensions of reviewers.
   Truman Capote

I have been aided by some censorious but able reviewers who were willing to take pains in order to inflict them.
   Frank Moore Colby

If critics want to help me, let them come sit next to me while I'm writing.
   Rita Mae Brown

The critic should describe, and not prescribe.
   Eugène Ionesco

The critic, to interpret his artist, even to understand his artist, must be able to get into the mind of his artist; he must feel and comprehend the vast pressure of the creative passion.
   H.L. Mencken

Critics of literature have the same essential function as teachers of literature: this is not to direct the judgment of the audience, but to assist the audience in those disciplines of reading on which any meaningful judgment must rest.
Mark Schorer

An important job of the critic is to savage what is mediocre or meretricious.
Susan Sontag

Critics sometimes appear to be addressing themselves to works other than those I remember writing.
Joyce Carol Oates

There is probably no hell for authors in the next world—they suffer so much from critics and publishers in this one.
C.N. Bovee

If the men of wit and genius would resolve never to complain in their works of critics and detractors, the next age would not know that they ever had any.
Jonathan Swift

I can imagine nothing more distressing to a critic than to have a writer see accurately into his own work.
Norman Mailer

The only really difficult thing about a poem is the critic's explanation of it.
Frank Moore Colby

When critics disagree, the artist is in accord with himself.
Oscar Wilde

Time is the only critic without ambition.
John Steinbeck

Mediocrity is more dangerous in a critic than in a writer.
Eugène Ionesco

Show me a critic without prejudices, and I'll show you an arrested cretin.
George Jean Nathan

The critic who justly admires all kinds of things simultaneously cannot love any one of them.
Max Beerbohm

For critics I care the five hundred thousandth part of the tythe of a half-farthing.
Charles Lamb

The lot of critics is to be remembered by what they failed to understand.
George Moore

There's an almost unavoidable feeling of smugness, of self-satisfaction, of teacher's pettishness, that sinks into a critic's bones.
Irwin Shaw

The best thing you can do about critics is never say a word. In the end you have the last say, and they know it.
  Tennessee Williams

Asking a working writer what he thinks about critics is like asking a lamppost what it feels about dogs.
  John Osborne

Criticism is the windows and chandeliers of art: it illuminates the enveloping darkness in which art might otherwise rest only vaguely discernible, and perhaps altogether unseen.
  George Jean Nathan

Criticism is prejudice made plausible.
  H.L. Mencken

Criticism is a study by which men grow important and formidable at very small expense.
  Samuel Johnson

Criticism is like champagne: nothing more execrable if bad, nothing more excellent if good.
  Charles Caleb Colton

Criticism is the art wherewith a critic tries to guess himself into a share of the artist's fame.
  George Jean Nathan

Pleasure is by no means an infallible critical guide, but it is the least fallible.
  W.H. Auden

I am bound by my own definition of criticism: a disinterested endeavor to learn and propagate the best that is known and thought is the world.
  Matthew Arnold

Scarcely any literature is so entirely unprofitable as the so-called criticism that overlays a pithy text with a windy sermon.
  John Morley

The avocation of assessing the failures of better men can be turned into a comfortable livelihood, providing you back it up with a Ph.D.
  Nelson Algren

Writing criticism is to writing fiction and poetry as hugging the shore is to sailing the open sea.
  John Updike

Tomes of aesthetic criticism hang on a few moments of real delight and intuition.
  George Santayana

A bad review by a man I admire hurts terribly.
  Anthony Burgess

Books should be tried by a judge and jury as though they were crimes.
   Samuel Butler

When a book is a good one and worth the price asked for it, the best thing for the reviewer to do is say so in plain words and have done.
   H.L. Mencken

A great deal of contemporary criticism reads to me like a man saying: "Of course I do not like green cheese; I am very fond of brown sherry."
   G.K. Chesterton

The main use in criticism is in showing what manner of man the critic is.
   Frank Moore Colby

I don't read my reviews, I measure them.
   Joseph Conrad

I love criticism just so long as it's unqualified praise.
   Noel Coward

I never read unpleasant things about myself.
   Truman Capote

The artists who want to be writers, read the reviews; the artists who want to write, don't.
   William Faulkner

I read very few critics. Friendly but ignorant reviews of my books tell me nothing. Hostile reviews can, for a brief time, irritate me. Favorable reviews by authors I treasure make me happy for a while. But if they are people who mean nothing to me, they depress me.
   Graham Greene

There is no reward so delightful, no pleasure so exquisite, as having one's work known and acclaimed by those whose applause confers honor.
   Molière

A unanimous chorus of approval is not an assurance of survival; authors who please everyone at once are quickly exhausted.
   André Gide

When a man publishes a book, there are so many stupid things said that he declares he'll never do it again. The praise is almost always worse than the criticism.
   Sherwood Anderson

There is no fate more distressing for an artist than to have to show himself off before fools, to see his work exposed to the criticism of the vulgar and ignorant.
   Molière

There is more ado to interpret interpretations than to interpret things, and more books upon books than upon any other subject; we do nothing but comment upon one another.
   Montaigne

I don't see how you can write anything of value if you don't offend someone.
  Marvin Harris

Reading reviews of your own book is . . . a no-win game. If the review is flattering, one tends to feel vain and uneasy. If it is bad, one tends to feel exposed, found out. Neither feeling does you any good.
  Walker Percy

It is advantageous to an author that his book should be attacked as well as praised. Fame is a shuttlecock. If it be struck at only one end of the room, it will soon fall to the ground. To keep it up, it must be struck at both ends.
  Samuel Johnson

You do not get a man's most effective criticism until you provoke him. Severe truth is expressed with some bitterness.
  Henry David Thoreau

The man who is asked by an author what he thinks of his work is not obliged to speak the truth.
  Samuel Johnson

People ask you for criticism but they only want praise.
  W. Somerset Maugham

You may scold a carpenter who has made you a bad table, though you cannot make a table. It is not your trade to make tables.
  Samuel Johnson

When I dislike what I see on the stage, I can be vastly amusing, but when I write about something I like, I am appallingly dull.
  Max Beerbohm

Your manuscript is both good and original; but the part that is good is not original, and the part that is original is not good.
  Samuel Johnson

When I have to praise a writer, I usually do it by attacking his enemies.
  H.L. Mencken

Criticism should not be querulous and wasting, all knife and root-puller, but guiding, instructive, inspiring, a south wind, not an east wind.
  Ralph Waldo Emerson

Confronted by an absolutely infuriating review it is sometimes helpful for the victim to do a little personal research on the critic. Is there any truth to the rumor that he had no formal education beyond the age of eleven? In any event, is he able to construct a simple English sentence? Do his participles dangle? When moved to lyricism does he write "I had a fun time"? Was he ever arrested for burglary? I don't know that you will prove anything this way, but it is perfectly harmless and quite soothing.
  Jean Kerr

One of the greatest creations of the human mind is the art of reviewing books without having to read them.
  G.C. Lichtenberg

I never read a book before reviewing it. It prejudices me so.
Sydney Smith

One cannot review a bad book without showing off.
W.H. Auden

Ideal dramatic criticism is unqualified appreciation.
Oscar Wilde

Honest criticism means nothing; what one wants is unrestrained passion,
fire for fire.
Henry Miller

I like criticism, but it must be my way.
Mark Twain

I don't care how unkind the things people say about me are so long as
they don't say them to my face.
Ogden Nash

I find criticism most instructive when an expert proves to me that my facts
or my grammar are wrong.
Vladimir Nabokov

You don't so much review a play as draw up a crushing brief against it.
Edmund Wilson

Taking to pieces is the trade of those who cannot construct.
Ralph Waldo Emerson

Anyone can be accurate and even profound, but it is damned hard work
to make criticism charming.
H.L. Mencken

Criticism can be instructive in the sense that it gives readers, including the
author of the book, some information about the critic's intelligence, or
honesty, or both.
Vladimir Nabokov

'Tis hard to say if greater want of skill
Appear in writing or judging ill.
Alexander Pope

We find fault with perfection itself.
Blaise Pascal

Reviewing has one advantage over suicide: in suicide you take it out of
yourself; in reviewing you take it out of other people.
George Bernard Shaw

Everything is infinitely fine, and any opinion is somehow coarser than the
texture of the real thing.
John Updike

Why did all these giants descend on me and my little stories? I wasn't
doing anything of national import. All I was trying to do was entertain
the public and make a buck.
Mickey Spillane

Every place swarms with commentaries; of authors there is great scarcity.
  Montaigne

Of all the cants which are canted in this canting world—though the cant of hypocrites may be the worst—the cant of criticism is the most tormenting.
  Laurence Sterne

Praise or blame has but a momentary effect on the man whose love of beauty in the abstract makes him a severe critic of his own works.
  John Keats

I cannot greatly care what the critics say of my work; if it is good, it will come to the surface in a generation or two and float, and if not, it will sink, having in the meantime provided me with a living, the opportunities of leisure, and a craftsman's intimate satisfactions.
  John Updike

Most critics write critiques which are by the authors they write critiques about. That would not be so bad, but then most authors write works which are by the critics who write critiques about them.
  Karl Kraus

You can't go around saying you're a writer if no one will take you seriously.
  William Kennedy

Literature is strewn with the wreckage of men who have minded beyond reason the opinion of others.
  Virginia Woolf

The slanders of the pen pierce to the heart; they rankle longest in the noblest spirits; they dwell ever present in the mind and render it morbidly sensitive to the most trifling collision.
  Washington Irving

The effects of notices upon novelists are well known to psychiatrists.
  H.L. Mencken

Real art has the capacity to make us nervous. By reducing the work of art to its content and then interpreting *that*, one tames the work of art.
  Susan Sontag

SELF-CRITICISM

Autocriticism does honor to the writer, dishonor to the critic.
Eugène Ionesco

If there is a special hell for writers, it would be in the forced contemplation of their own works.
John Dos Passos

I don't think many writers like their best-known piece of work, particularly when it was written a long time ago.
Lillian Hellman

If my books had been any worse I would not have been invited to Hollywood, and if they had been any better I would not have come.
Raymond Chandler

There are writers whose gift is to make terribly complicated things simple. But I know my gift is the reverse: to take relatively simple things and complicate them to the point of madness. But there you are: one learns who one is, and it is at one's peril that one attempts to become someone else.
John Barth

I am always at a loss to know how much to believe of my own stories.
Washington Irving

The books I haven't written are better than the books other people have.
Cyril Connolly

I'm a manufacturer of stories.
Mickey Spillane

I will not buy a magazine that will publish what I write.
Goodman Ace

I'm a lousy writer; a helluva lot of people have got lousy taste.
Grace Metalious

CENSORSHIP

The dirtiest book of all is the expurgated book.
  Walt Whitman

The books that the world calls immoral are the books that show the world its own shame.
  Oscar Wilde

Give me the liberty to know, to utter, and to argue freely according to conscience, above all liberties.
  John Milton

No member of society has a right to teach any doctrine contrary to what society holds to be true.
  Samuel Johnson

Nobody is more dangerous than he who imagines himself pure in heart; for his purity, by definition, is unassailable.
  James Baldwin

Persons who undertake to pry into, or cleanse out all the filth of a common sewer, either cannot have very nice noses, or will soon lose them.
  William Hazlitt

Men fear thought as they fear nothing else on earth—more than ruin, more even than death.
  Bertrand Russell

Knowledge cannot defile, nor consequently the books, if the will and conscience be not defiled.
  John Milton

Those whom books will hurt will not be proof against events. If some books are deemed more baneful and their sale forbid, how, then, with deadlier facts, not dreams of doting men? Events, not books, should be forbid.
  Herman Melville

Men in earnest have no time to waste
In patching fig-leaves for the naked truth.
  James Russell Lowell

Censorship is an excuse to talk about sex.
  Fran Lebowitz

Assassination is the extreme form of censorship.
  George Bernard Shaw

PUBLICITY

No writer, especially a young and unknown writer, resents publicity of
any kind—whatever he may say.
  Kingsley Amis

If you write one book and then go on to another, readers pay half attention to the book and half attention to the publicity. Without publicity you
lose the sense of an audience that has learned how to read you, or not.
Everyone waits not so much for the book as for the essays and talk about
the book.
  Harold Brodkey

I've had enough publicity to last an army of super rats. I don't know
anybody who gets as much publicity as I do for doing nothing.
  Truman Capote

Notoriety and public confession in literary form is a frazzler of the heart
you were born with, believe me.
  Jack Kerouac

It's much more important to write than to be written about.
  Gabriel Garcia Márquez

In my district of Gascony, it is thought a joke to see me in print. The further from my home the knowledge of me travels, the higher I am valued.
  Montaigne

If a writer proclaims himself as isolated, uninfluenced and responsible to
no one, he should not be surprised if he is ignored, uninfluential, and perceived as irresponsible.
  Charles Newman

It is very pleasant to be written up, even by a writer.
  Joyce Cary

To promote a book you are expected to get it up eight or ten times a day,
sometimes in Philadelphia.
  Roy Blount, Jr.

A boy has to peddle his book.
  Truman Capote

FAME

Fame is a fickle food
Upon a shifting plate.
    Emily Dickinson

Fame is a vapor, popularity an accident; the only earthly certainty is oblivion.
    Mark Twain

Fame isn't a thing. It's a feeling. Like what you get after a pill.
    Joyce Cary

Fame is a bee
It has a song—
It has a sting—
Ah, too, it has a wing.
    Emily Dickinson

Fame is a constant effort.
    Jules Renard

Fame is proof that people are gullible.
    Ralph Waldo Emerson

I want it.
    Tobi Sanders

First you're unknown, then you write one book and you move up to obscurity.
    Martin Myers

A writer is always admired most, not by those who have read him, but by those who have merely heard about him.
    H.L. Mencken

Enduring fame is promised only to those writers who can offer to successive generations a substance constantly renewed; for every generation arrives upon the scene with its own particular hunger.
    André Gide

When audiences come to see us authors lecture, it is largely in the hope that we'll be funnier to look at than to read.
Sinclair Lewis

It took me fifteen years to discover I had no talent for writing, but I couldn't give it up because by that time I was too famous.
Robert Benchley

Lolita is famous, not I. I am an obscure, double obscure, novelist with an unpronounceable name.
Vladimir Nabokov

Odd things happen to book writers when they become famous.
Ronald Sukenick

Fill an author with a titanic fame and you do not make him titanic; you often merely burst him.
Frank Moore Colby

Fame lies in being able to do what I like … The Académie Française and the renown of being a great writer—this great crown, so to speak, permits me to wear, in season and out of season and wherever I choose, my old gray felt hat. If I wanted, I could go to the opera in slippers.
Anatole France

Early acclaim won't harm a writer if he has the strength, or the cynicism, not to believe in that acclaim.
Martin Amis

In my district of Gascony, it is thought a joke to see me in print. The further from my home the knowledge of me travels, the higher I am valued.
Montaigne

Little presses write to me for manuscripts and when I write back that I haven't any, they write to ask if they can print the letter saying I haven't any.
John Steinbeck

All this talk about ourselves, all these symposiums and pronouncements—sometimes I have the feeling that everybody is out reading the interviews and nobody's at home with the novels.
Philip Roth

If I could I would always work in silence and obscurity, and let my efforts be known by their results.
Emily Brontë

Writers should be read—but neither seen nor heard.
Daphne du Maurier

One should never be known by sight.
Henry Green

Fame ... has made me the observed instead of the observer. Bad for a
writer.
    Ken Kesey

I like to be able to listen to conversations without people turning around
to look at me over their shoulders. I want to be the man behind you in
the fish shop.
    Len Deighton

I don't mind being recognized—it's part of the business.
    Mickey Spillane

It's a short walk from the halleleujah to the hoot.
    Vladimir Nabokov

SUCCESS

Success comes to a writer, as a rule, so gradually that it is always something of a shock to him to look back and realize the heights to which he has climbed.
  P.G. Wodehouse

As far as I can tell, the only healthy attitude for a writer is to consider praise, blame, book chat, and table position at Elaine's irrelevant to the writing, and to get on with it.
  Jay McInerney

Success is feminine and like a woman; if you cringe before her she will override you. So the way to treat her is to show her the back of your hand. Then maybe she will do the crawling.
  William Faulkner

Success is like a horrible disaster, worse than a fire in one's home. Fame consumes the home of the soul.
  Malcolm Lowry

Literary success of any enduring kind is made by refusing to do what publishers want, by refusing to write what the public wants, by refusing to accept any popular standard, by refusing to write anything to order.
  Lafcadio Hearn

Success and failure are both difficult to endure. Along with success come drugs, divorce, fornication, bullying, travel, meditation, medication, depression, neurosis and suicide. With failure comes failure.
  Joseph Heller

I think what's most disturbing about success is that it's very hazardous to your health, as well as to your daily routine. Not only are there intrusions on your time, but there is a kind of corrosion of your own humility and sense of necessary workmanship. You get the idea that anything you do is in some way marvelous.
  John Updike

In other countries, art and literature are left to a lot of shabby bums living in attics and feeding on booze and spaghetti, but in America the successful writer or picture-painter is indistinguishable from any other decent business man.
  Sinclair Lewis

The rarest thing in literature, and the only success, is when the author disappears and his work remains.
  François Mauriac

If your first book is a smash, your second book gets kicked in the face.
  John Berryman

Failure is very difficult for a writer to bear, but very few can manage the shock of early success.
  Maurice Valency

Of all the enemies of literature, success is the most insidious.
  Cyril Connolly

I detest and despise success, yet I cannot do without it. I am like a drug addict—if nobody talks about me for a couple of months I have withdrawal symptoms.
  Eugène Ionesco

Success and failure are equally disastrous.
  Tennessee Williams

BEST-SELLERS

A best-seller is the gilded tomb of a mediocre talent.
Logan Pearsall Smith

Best-Sellerism is the star system of the book world. A "best-seller" is a celebrity among books. It is known primarily (sometimes exclusively) for its well-knownness.
Daniel J. Boorstin

Can anybody be so naive as to think he or she can learn anything about the past from those buxom best-sellers that are hawked around by book clubs under the heading of historical novels?
Vladimir Nabokov

The writing of a best-seller represents only a fraction of the total effort required to create one.
Ted Nicholas

If we should ever inaugurate a hall of fame, it would be reserved exclusively and hopefully for authors who, having written four bestsellers, *still refrained* from starting out on a lecture tour.
E.B. White

A best-seller was a book which somehow sold well simply because it was selling well.
Daniel J. Boorstin

The principle of procrastinated rape is said to be the ruling one in all the great best-sellers.
V.S. Pritchett

MONEY

Sir, no man but a blockhead ever wrote except for money.
  Samuel Johnson

Instead of marvelling with Johnson, how anything but profit should incite
men to literary labour, I am rather surprised that mere emolument should
induce them to labour so well.
  Thomas Green

Write out of love; write out of instinct; write out of reason. But always
for money.
  Louis Untermeyer

Write without pay until somebody offers pay; if nobody offers within
three years, sawing wood is what you were intended for.
  Mark Twain

Money to a writer is time to write.
  Frank Herbert

If I had money I'd never write.
  Louis-Ferdinand Céline

I only write when I need the money. I hate to work. If I got enough
money, I don't write. What's the sense of making it if you can't spend it?
  Mickey Spillane

I've never written a book because there's going to be a lot of money in it,
because I know that's the surest way to take five years off your life.
  Norman Mailer

If they didn't pay me, I'd do it for nothing.
  Laurel Goldman

The financial rewards just don't make up for the expenditure of energy,
the damage to health caused by stimulants and narcotics, the fear that
one's work isn't good enough. I think, if I had enough money, I'd give up
writing tomorrow.
  Anthony Burgess

The way I've operated with publishers is that I live on the future. I take as much money as I can get for as long as I can get it, you know, a year or two years, and by the end of that time your credit begins to have holes in it, and—well, you have to come up.
  Nelson Algren

Starting with a very modest advance from my publisher, I rose to near-millionaire status, then plummeted to my current state of affairs, which recently saw me borrow a few dollars from my father to fix the muffler on my car—all in eight years.
  Philip Caputo

For hundreds of years, writers have been giving it away like warmhearted country girls in the big city, and it is not astonishing that their lovers (that is, the publishers) balk at giving a mink coat when a pair of nylons will do the job.
  Mario Puzo

There is a great discovery still to be made in literature—that of paying literary men by the quantity they do not write.
  Thomas Carlyle

Almost anyone can be an author; the business is to collect money and fame from this state of being.
  A.A. Milne

I should like to see the custom introduced of readers who are pleased with a book sending the author some small cash token: anything between half-a-crown and a hundred pounds. . . . Not more than a hundred pounds—that would be bad for my character—not less than half-a-crown—that would do no good to yours.
  Cyril Connolly

When you are really frantic and worried about money, you find that if it's going to be a question of writing to live, why, you just damn well buckle to and do it.
  Lawrence Durrell

Writing is the hardest way of earning a living, with the possible exception of wrestling alligators.
  Olin Miller

If writers were good businessmen, they'd have too much sense to be writers.
  Irvin S. Cobb

The profession of book-writing makes horse racing seem like a solid, stable business.
  John Steinbeck

Writing is the only profession where no one considers you ridiculous if you earn no money.
  Jules Renard

Modern poets write against business, but all of us write for money.
Robert Frost

Poetry has never brought me in enough money to buy shoestrings.
William Wordsworth

Poets are terribly sensitive people, and one of the things they are most sensitive about is cash.
Robert Penn Warren

Money is a kind of poetry.
Wallace Stevens

There's no money in poetry, but then there's no poetry in money either.
Robert Graves

I'd like to have money. And I'd like to be a good writer. These two can come together, and I hope they will, but if that's too adorable, I'd rather have money.
Dorothy Parker

The dubious privilege of a freelance writer is he's given the freedom to starve anywhere.
S.J. Perelman

The advance for a book should be at least as much as the cost of the lunch at which it was discussed.
Calvin Trillin

I hope you get as much pleasure reading my book as I got spending the money you paid me for it.
Dan Poynter

The writings by which one can live are not the writings which themselves live.
John Stuart Mill

The two most beautiful words in the English language are "Check enclosed."
Dorothy Parker

Years ago, to say you were a writer was not the highest recommendation to your landlord. Today, he at least hesitates before he refuses to rent you an apartment—for all he knows you may be rich.
Arthur Miller

You must not suppose, because I am a man of letters, that I ever tried to earn an honest living.
George Bernard Shaw

You must avoid giving hostages to fortune, like getting an expensive wife, an expensive house, and a style of living that never lets you afford the time to take the chance to write what you wish.
Irwin Shaw

Being in a garret doesn't do you any good unless you're some sort of a Keats.
   Dorothy Parker

I've only spent about ten per cent of my energies on writing. The other ninety per cent went to keeping my head above water.
   Katherine Anne Porter

For me the main pleasure of having money is being able to afford as many completely retyped drafts as I like.
   Gore Vidal

Money gives one time to rewrite books until they're "done"—or abandoned.
   Gore Vidal

Even if I could not earn a penny from my writing, I would earn my livelihood at something else and continue to write at night.
   Irving Wallace

There is only one genuinely ghastly thing hack jobs do to writers, and that is to waste their precious time.
   Kurt Vonnegut

I never write *metropolis* for seven cents because I can get the same price for *city*. I never write *policeman* because I can get the same money for *cop*.
   Mark Twain

Syntax is my bread and butter.
   Roy Blount, Jr.

You can survive as a writer on hustle: you get paid very little for each piece, but you write a lot of pieces. Christ, I did book reviews—I did anything. It was $85 here, $110 there—I was like Molly Bloom: "Yes I will, yes I will, yes." Whatever anybody wanted done, I did it.
   Kurt Vonnegut

Why is it that an inventor can sit in a room for five years with a sheet of paper and a pencil, and when he finally comes up with something, it's capital gain; but when writers do the same thing, it's current income, which is heavily taxed?
   Adam Smith

Writing is the most wonderful and satisfying task in the world, but it does have one or two insignificant flaws. Among those flaws is the fact that a writer can almost never make a living at it.
   Isaac Asimov

HOLLYWOOD

I went out there for a thousand a week, and I worked Monday, and I got fired Wednesday. The guy that hired me was out of town Tuesday.
   Nelson Algren

A dreary industrial town controlled by hoodlums of enormous wealth, the ethical sense of a pack of jackals, and taste so degraded that it befouled everything it touched.
   S.J. Perelman

Hollywood is a trip through a sewer in a glass-bottomed boat.
   Wilson Mizner

I'm a Hollywood writer; so I put on a sports jacket and take off my brain.
   Ben Hecht

Hollywood has the finest brains in the world out there. But they're up against all these vested interests, and vested interests are the very devil for the artist.
   Frank O'Connor

My principal feeling about Hollywood is suicide. If I could get out of bed and into the shower, I was all right. Since I never paid the bills, I'd reach for the phone and order the most elaborate breakfast I could think of, and then I'd try to make it to the shower before I hanged myself.
   John Cheever

The only -*ism* Hollywood believes in is plagiarism.
   Dorothy Parker

It was a hideous and untenable place when I dwelt there, populated with few exceptions by Yahoos, and now that it has become the chief citadel of television, it's unspeakable.
   S.J. Perelman

Hollywood money isn't money. It's congealed snow, melts in your hand, and there you are.
   Dorothy Parker

All Hollywood corrupts, and absolute Hollywood corrupts absolutely.
   Edmund Wilson

COMPETITION

I don't feel in competition with other writers. Because I don't write about the same things as any other writer that I know of does.
Truman Capote

Each writer is a separate entity. The mistake people like Mailer make is that writing is for him a track race.
William Styron

Publishing is a horse race. And you can't not worry whether your horse will win, place, or show. The rate of sale counts. I respect my competition. Being number one can mean the difference between selling 49 and 50 copies in a single bookstore.
Judith Krantz

I think about Tolstoy, Flaubert and Dickens, and I'm jealous of what those authors accomplished. Because I am jealous, I am a writer now. I remain jealous and this gives me a guide to what I might accomplish.
James Michener

I started out very quiet and I beat Mr. Turgenev. Then I trained hard and I beat Mr. de Maupassant. I've fought two draws with Mr. Stendhal, and I think I had an edge in the last one. But nobody's going to get me in any ring with Mr. Tolstoy unless I'm crazy or I keep getting better.
Ernest Hemingway

I can write better than anyone who can write faster, and I can write faster than anyone who can write better.
A.J. Liebling

Your battle is not with other authors, your battle is with what you put on the paper.
J.P. Donleavy

I cannot think that Real Poets have any competition. None are greatest in the Kingdom of Heaven; it is so in Poetry.
William Blake

Writing. . .is practically the only activity a person can do that is not competitive.
Paul Theroux

COLLEAGUES

The language of Aristophanes reeks of his miserable quackery: it is made up of the lowest and most miserable puns; he doesn't even please the people, and to men of judgment and honor he is intolerable; his arrogance is insufferable, and all honest men detest his malice.
   Plutarch

A cliché anthologist . . . and maker of ragamuffin manikins.
   Aristophanes on Euripides

The graces once made up their mind
A shrine inviolate to find:
And thus they found, and that with ease,
The soul of Aristophanes.
   Plato

Cicero's style bores me. When I have spent an hour reading him. . . and try to recollect what I have extracted, I usually find it nothing but wind.
   Montaigne

Seneca I've never been able to take seriously. I've always thought that he really belonged in the old-time Hearst Sunday supplement, or in one of the lower order of fantasy and science fiction magazines.
   Kenneth Rexroth

Dante makes me sick.
   Lope de Vega

I'll bet Shakespeare compromised himself a lot; anybody who's in the entertainment industry does to some extent.
   Christopher Isherwood

Shakespeare never has six lines together without a fault.
   Samuel Johnson

Shakespeare was a dramatist of note;
He lived by writing things to quote.
   H.C. Bunner

If Bacon wrote Shakespeare, who wrote Bacon?
   George Lyman Kittredge

I don't know if Bacon wrote the works of Shakespeare, but if he did not, he missed the opportunity of his life.
  James M. Barrie

If the public likes you, you're good. Shakespeare was a common, down-to-earth writer in his day.
  Mickey Spillane

Macbeth is a tale told by a genius, full of soundness and fury, signifying many things.
  James Thurber

To this day I cannot read *King Lear*, having had the advantage of studying it accurately in school.
  Alfred North Whitehead

Poets like Shakespeare knew more about psychiatry than any $25-an-hour man.
  Robert Frost

He took all his plots from old novels, and threw their stories into a dramatic shape, at as little expense of thought as you or I could turn his plays back again into prose tales.
  Lord Byron on William Shakespeare

To know the force of human genius we should read Shakespeare; to see the insignificance of human learning we may study his commentators.
  William Hazlitt

To read Dryden, Pope, etc., you need only count syllables; but to read Donne you must measure *time*, and discover the time of each word by the sense of passion.
  Samuel Taylor Coleridge

I have not wasted my life trifling with literary fools in taverns as Jonson did when he should have been shaking England with the thunder of his spirit.
  George Bernard Shaw.

George Wither was taken prisoner, and was in danger of his life, having written severely against the king. Sir John Denham went to the king, and desired his majesty not to hang him, for that whilst G.W. lived he should not be the worst poet in England.
  John Aubrey

His imagination resembles the wings of an ostrich.
  Thomas Babington Macaulay on John Dryden

Steele might become a reasonably good writer if he would pay a little more attention to grammar, learn something about the propriety and dispostion of words and, incidentally, get some information on the subject he intends to handle.
  Jonathan Swift on Richard Steele

Pope came off clean with Homer; but they say
Broome went before, and kindly swept the way.
  J. Henley

His more ambitious works may be defined as careless thinking carefully versified.
  James Russell Lowell on Alexander Pope

You have but two subjects, yourself and me. I am sick of both.
  Samuel Johnson to James Boswell

That he was a coxcomb and a bore, weak, vain, pushing, curious, garrulous, was obvious to all who were acquainted with him. That he could not reason, that he had not wit, no humor, nor eloquence, is apparent from his writings . . . Nature had made him a slave and an idolater. His mind resembled those creepers which the botanists call parasites and which can subsist only by clinging round the stems and imbibing the juices of stronger plants.
  Thomas Babington Macaulay on James Boswell

Schiller's blank verse is bad. He moves in it as a fly in a glue bottle. His thoughts have their connection and variety, it is true, but there is no sufficiently corresponding movement in the verse.
  Samuel Taylor Coleridge

In his youth, Wordsworth sympathized with the French Revolution, went to France, wrote good poetry and had a natural daughter. At this period, he was a "bad" man. Then he became "good," abandoned his daughter, adopted correct principles and wrote bad poetry.
  Bertrand Russell

Carlyle is the same old sausage, fizzing and sputtering in his own grease.
  Henry James

[Edward] Gibbon's style is detestable; but is not the worst thing about him.
  Samuel Taylor Coleridge

From the poetry of Lord Byron they drew a system of ethics compounded of misanthropy and voluptuosness—a system in which the two greatest commandments were to hate your neighbor and to love your neighbor's wife.
  Thomas Babington Macaulay

That dirty little blackguard.
  Lord Byron on John Keats

I became interested in syphilis when I worked for a time at a mental hospital full of GPI cases. I discovered there was a correlation between the spirochete and mad talent. The tubercule also produces a lyrical drive. Keats had both.
  Anthony Burgess

Such writing is mental masturbation—he is always fr-gg-g his Imagination. I don't mean he is indecent, but viciously soliciting his own ideas into a state, which is neither poetry nor anything else but a Bedlam vision produced by raw pork and opium.
    Lord Byron on John Keats

Shelley I saw once. His voice was the most obnoxious squeak I ever was tormented with.
    Charles Lamb

He was a liar and a cheat; he paid no regard to truth, nor to any kind of moral obligation.
    Robert Southey on Percy Bysshe Shelley

A hoary-headed and toothless baboon.
    Thomas Carlyle on Ralph Waldo Emerson

Tennyson was an appalling exhibitionist. He thought of himself as a combination of Homer and Sir Henry Irving. He used to go swaggering along country lanes reciting aloud and swinging a cloak. He had an almost theatrically pink complexion and two red spots on his cheeks. I think he used makeup.
    Bertrand Russell

Tennyson is a beautiful half of a poet.
    Ralph Waldo Emerson

Gogol was a strange creature.
    Vladimir Nabokov

Heinrich Heine so loosened the corsets of the German language that today every little salesman can fondle her breasts.
    Karl Kraus

To me, Poe's prose is unreadable—like Jane Austen's. No, there is a difference. I would read his prose on a salary, but not Jane's.
    Mark Twain

Mr. Whitman's muse is at once indecent and ugly, lascivious and gawky, lubricious and coarse.
    Lafcadio Hearn

Thoreau's quality is very penetrating and contagious; reading him is like eating onions—one must look out or the flavor will reach his own page.
    John Burroughs

An agile but unintelligent and abnormal German, possessed of the mania of grandeur.
    Leo Tolstoy on Friedrich Wilhelm Nietzsche

When you read Turgenev, you know you are reading Turgenev. When you read Tolstoy, you read just because you cannot stop.
    Vladimir Nabokov

Rilke was the greatest Lesbian poet since Sappho.
  W.H. Auden

A village explainer, excellent if you were a village, but if you were not, not.
  Gertrude Stein on Ezra Pound

I am seldom interested in what he is saying, but only in the way he says it.
  T.S. Eliot on Ezra Pound

T.S. Eliot owes almost everything to Pound.
  Truman Capote

Both T.S. Eliot and I like to play, but I like to play euchre, while he likes to play Eucharist.
  Robert Frost

The cruelest thing that has happened to Lincoln since he was shot by Booth was to fall into the hands of Carl Sandburg.
  Edmund Wilson

The high-water mark, so to speak, of Socialist literature is W.H. Auden, a sort of gutless Kipling.
  George Orwell

I am fairly unrepentant about her poetry. I really think that three quarters of it is gibberish. However, I must crush down these thoughts otherwise the dove of peace will shit on me.
  Noel Coward on Edith Sitwell

So you've been reviewing Edith Sitwell's latest piece of virgin dung, have you? Isn't she a poisonous thing of a woman, lying, concealing, flipping, plagiarizing, misquoting and being as clever a crooked literary publicist as ever?
  Dylan Thomas

Williams' poems in the main fatigue me severely.
  H.L. Mencken

If it were thought that anything I wrote was influenced by Robert Frost, I would take that particular work of mine, shred it, and flush it down the toilet, hoping not to clog the pipes. A more sententious, holding-forth old bore who expected every hero-worshiping adenoidal little twerp of a student-poet to hang on his every word I never saw.
  James Dickey

He was a very mean man. Everybody that ever knew him at all will tell you that.
  Truman Capote on Robert Frost

Dylan Thomas once told me that poets only know two kinds of birds by sight; one is a robin and the other a seagull, he said, and the rest of them he had to look up.
  Lawrence Durrell

He's the only poet that I've ever known in the universe who simply did not drink.
John Berryman on Randall Jarrell

I find it distressing to remember that this writer of genius regularly compared herself with writers who were in no way her peers and was upset by their success and longed for a certain kind of commercial success which was so much less than what she deserved.
Susan Sontag on Sylvia Plath

Yevtushenko has. . .an ego that can crack crystal at a distance of twenty feet.
John Cheever

Poets, like whores, are only hated by each other.
William Wycherley

My heroes are poets. I have rejoiced in the privilege, unearned, of spending evenings with Eliot, days and weeks with Auden, occasions with Cocteau, hours with Dylan Thomas, Robert Graves, Robert Lowell, Joseph Brodsky, Eugenio Montale, Ingeborg Bachmann. I venerate them all.
Robert Craft

He has occasional flashes of silence that make his conversation perfectly delightful.
Sydney Smith on Thomas Babington Macaulay

A glittering humbug.
Thomas Carlyle on Victor Hugo

Victor Hugo is the greatest French poet, alas.
André Gide

Victor Hugo was a madman who thought he was Victor Hugo.
Jean Cocteau

It was quite fashionable to poke fun at Hugo.
Eugène Ionesco

One must have a heart of stone to read the death of Little Nell by Dickens without laughing.
Oscar Wilde

Dickens was the incarnation of cockneydom, a caricaturist who aped the moralist; he should have kept to short stories. If his novels are read at all in the future people will wonder what we saw in him.
George Meredith

The four greatest novelists the world has ever known—Balzac, Dickens, Tolstoy and Dostoevski—wrote their respective languages very badly.
W. Somerset Maugham

In my opinion, the writers of English who most clearly use the correct word every time and who most artfully and deftly put together their sentences and paragraphs are Charles Dickens, Mark Twain, and P.G. Wodehouse.
    Isaac Asimov

His style is chaos, illuminated by flashes of lightning. As a writer he has mastered everything except language; as a novelist he can do everything except tell a story; as an artist he is everything, except articulate.
    Oscar Wilde on George Meredith

I do not like this trick his characters have of "sinning their way to Jesus."
    Vladimir Nabokov on Fyodor Dostoevski

Poor Matt, he's gone to Heaven, no doubt—but he won't like God.
    Robert Louis Stevenson on Matthew Arnold

Can't understand Rimbaud at all.
    Joseph Conrad

His work is evil, and he is one of those unhappy beings of whom one can say that it would have been better had he never been born.
    Anatole France on Émile Zola

M. Zola is determined to show that, if he has not got genius, he can at least be dull.
    Oscar Wilde

Henry James had a mind so fine that no idea could violate it.
    T.S. Eliot

Henry James was one of the nicest old ladies I ever met.
    William Faulkner

An idiot, and a Boston idiot, to boot, than which there is nothing lower in the world.
    H.L. Mencken on Henry James

Mr. Henry James writes fiction as if it were a painful duty.
    Oscar Wilde

I loved him, was frightened by him, was bored by him, was staggered by his wisdom and stupefied by his intricacies . . . I was sometimes so bored that I had pins and needles in my legs and arms.
    Hugh Walpole on Henry James

I am reading Henry James . . . and feel myself as one entombed in a block of smooth amber.
    Virginia Woolf

Poor Henry, he's spending eternity wandering round and round a stately park and the fence is just too high for him to peep over and they're having tea just too far away for him to hear what the Countess is saying.
    W. Somerset Maugham

Henry James would have been vastly improved as a novelist by a few whiffs from the Chicago stockyards.
   H.L. Mencken

I have the reputation of having read all of Henry James. Which would argue a misspent youth *and* middle age.
   James Thurber

He festooned the dung heap on which he had placed himself with sonnets as people grow honeysuckle around outdoor privies.
   Quentin Crisp on Oscar Wilde

What a tiresome, affected sod.
   Noel Coward on Oscar Wilde

You have to be over thirty to enjoy Proust.
   Gore Vidal

I was reading Proust for the first time. Very poor stuff. I think he was mentally defective.
   Evelyn Waugh

Mr. Conrad has paid us a pretty compliment by learning to write the English language correctly, and the journalists are so pleased that they have assigned him a place in our literature.
   George Moore

He wasn't exactly hostile to facts, but he was apathetic about them.
   Wolcott Gibbs on Alexander Woollcott

He became mellow before he became ripe.
   Alexander Woollcott on Christopher Morley

Bernard Shaw has no enemies but is intensely disliked by his friends.
   Oscar Wilde

It is his life work to announce the obvious in terms of the scandalous.
   H.L. Mencken on George Bernard Shaw

Mr. Shaw is (I suspect) the only man on earth who has never written any poetry.
   G.K. Chesterton

The more I think you over the more it comes home to me what an unmitigated Middle Victorian ass you are!
   H.G. Wells to George Bernard Shaw

Inconceivable as it may seem, I found Shaw an awful bore.
   H.G. Wells

Nobody can read Freud without realizing that he was the scientific equivalent of another nuisance, George Bernard Shaw.
   Robert Maynard Hutchins

He writes his plays for the ages—the ages between five and twelve.
   George Jean Nathan on George Bernard Shaw

H.L. Mencken suffers from the hallucination that he is H.L. Mencken—there is no cure for a disease of that magnitude.
Maxwell Bodenheim

She had a great sense of humor. Very malicious.
May Sarton on Virginia Woolf

Kafka was possessed by...inhibitions. They impeded him in everything he did—in sex as well as in writing. He craved love and fled from it. He wrote a sentence and immediately crossed it out.
Isaac Bashevis Singer

I like him, but one Kafka in a century is enough.
Isaac Bashevis Singer

The greatest female writer in America now—but just wait until next year.
Carson McCullers on Katherine Anne Porter

His best work was done before he became successful.
H.L. Mencken on Theodore Dreiser

Hammett took murder out of the parlor and put it in the alley where it belongs.
Raymond Chandler

His style has the desperate jauntiness of an orchestra fiddling away for dear life on a sinking ship.
Edmund Wilson on Evelyn Waugh

You should approach Joyce's *Ulysses* as the illiterate Baptist preacher approaches the Old Testament: with faith.
William Faulkner

James Joyce—an essentially private man who wished his total indifference to public notice to be universally recognized.
Tom Stoppard

My God, what a clumsy olla putrida James Joyce is! Nothing but old fags and cabbage stumps of quotations from the Bible and the rest, stewed in the juice of deliberate, journalistic dirty-mindedness.
D.H. Lawrence

English literature's performing flea.
Sean O'Casey on P.G. Wodehouse

Your novel has every fault the English novel can have...a rotten work of genius.
Ford Madox Ford to D.H. Lawrence

Fraud Madox Fraud.
Osbert Sitwell

I loathe you. You revolt me stewing in your consumption...the Italians were quite right to have nothing to do with you. You are a loathesome reptile—I hope you will die.
D.H. Lawrence to Katherine Mansfield

Rebecca West: I've never been able to do just one draft. Do you know anyone who can?
Interviewer: I think D.H. Lawrence did.
Rebecca West: You could often tell.

He would not blow his nose without moralizing on conditions in the handkerchief industry.
    Cyril Connolly on George Orwell

He couldn't write for toffee, bless his heart.
    Rebecca West on W. Somerset Maugham

I was in love with her.
    May Sarton on Elizabeth Bowen

He liked women writers and I don't think he ever had a true interest in a woman who wasn't a writer—an odd turn-on indeed and one I've noticed not greatly shared.
    Elizabeth Hardwick on Robert Lowell

Sherwood Anderson never tried to please anybody—he considered it everybody's duty to please him.
    Ben Hecht

Gertrude Stein's prose is a cold, black suet-pudding. We can represent it as a cold suet-roll of fabulously reptilian length. Cut it at any point, it is...the same heavy, sticky, opaque mass all through, and all along.
    Percy Wyndham Lewis

Miss Stein was a past master at making nothing happen very slowly.
    Clifton Fadiman

It's a shame you never knew her before she went to pot. You know a funny thing, she never could write dialogue.
    Ernest Hemingway on Gertrude Stein

Hemingway? What did he do that made him so big? He wrote some good stuff, but what was so *big* about it? He never sold that many.
    Mickey Spillane

Hemingway's remarks are not literature.
    Gertrude Stein

I read him for the first time in the early forties, something about bells, balls and bulls, and loathed it.
    Vladimir Nabokov on Ernest Hemingway

He was an incredibly vain man.
    John Steinbeck on Ernest Hemingway

Hemingway had the bad habit of never forgiving anyone for giving him a hand up.
    Malcolm Cowley

When his cock wouldn't stand up, he blew his head off. He sold himself a line of bullshit and bought it.
    Germaine Greer on Ernest Hemingway

He was the critics' darling because he never changed style, theme nor story. He made no experiments in thinking nor emotion.
    John Steinbeck on Ernest Hemingway

Hemingway was a necromancer who adopted every superior Balzacian trick in the book, each technical device that Flaubert and Tolstoy and Dickens had found useful, so that quite often his work seemed better than it really was.
    James Michener

I detest him, but I was certainly under his spell when I was very young, as we all were. I thought his prose was perfect—until I read Stephen Crane and realized where he got it from.
    Gore Vidal on Ernest Hemingway

Hemingway had a remarkable interest in and understanding of homosexuality, for a man who wasn't a homosexual.
    Tennessee Williams

There was a mean man.
    Truman Capote on Ernest Hemingway

Thomas Wolfe has always seemed to me the most overrated, long-winded and boring of reputable American novelists.
    Edith Oliver

I knew Wolfe slightly. He was a very amiable fellow, but he always seemed to me to be almost as confused as Sherwood Anderson.
    H.L. Mencken on Thomas Wolfe

If it must be Thomas, let it be Mann, and if it must be Wolfe let it be Nero, but never let it be Thomas Wolfe.
    Peter De Vries

Beckett writes short but exquisite things.
    Pablo Neruda

He writes by sanded fingertips.
    Lillian Hellman on Tennessee Williams

Every word she wrote was a lie, including "and" and "the."
    Mary McCarthy on Lillian Hellman

Odets, where is thy sting?
    George S. Kaufman

The only man who wrote a great deal in our time was John O'Hara, because he went on the wagon and had nothing else to do.
    Irwin Shaw

Hard to lay down but easy not to pick up.
    Malcolm Cowley on John O'Hara's novels

You know the beginning of *Gatsby*, the little frontispiece? They say Fitzgerald made that up. I always thought that was such a great thing to do—make up a quote and pretend it really inspired you.
   Nora Ephron

Faulkner said more asinine things than any other major American writer. I can't remember a single interesting remark Faulkner ever made.
   Norman Mailer

Faulkner had a mean small Southern streak in him, and most of his pronunciamentos reflect that meanness. He's a great writer, but he's not all that interesting in most of his passing remarks.
   Norman Mailer

Could Faulkner find a publisher now?
   Annie Dillard

I knew Faulkner very well. He was a great friend of mine. Well, as much as you could be a friend of his, unless you were a fourteen-year-old nymphet.
   Truman Capote

He's a plowboy in prose style, but the spiritual struggle is there. You can feel the alcohol in the bloodstream.
   Lawrence Durrell on William Faulkner

Capote should be heard, not read.
   Gore Vidal

Like Toulouse-Lautrec, he will come to represent his period, and he will be treasured for the masterly way he epitomized it.
   James Michener on Truman Capote

Truman is canny as hell, but he's not the brightest guy in the world.
   Norman Mailer

He thinks he's Bunny Mellon.
   Gore Vidal on Truman Capote

A Republican housewife from Kansas with all the prejudices.
   Gore Vidal on Truman Capote

He was a full-fledged master of the language before he was old enough to vote.
   William Styron on Truman Capote

Truman Capote has made lying an art. A *minor* art.
   Gore Vidal

I think you judge Truman a bit too charitably when you call him a child: he is more like a sweetly vicious old lady.
   Tennessee Williams

We European innocents think of Truman Capote mainly as a writer. I know he is seen otherwise in America.
   John Fowles

He'd be all right if he took his finger out of his mouth.
  Harold Robbins on Truman Capote

He's a second-rate Stephen Birmingham. And Steven Birmingham is third-rate.
  Truman Capote on Louis Auchincloss

I'm told, on very good authority, that he hasn't stopped writing at all. That he's written at least five or six short novels and that all of them have been turned down by *The New Yorker*. And that all of them are very strange and about Zen Buddhism.
  Truman Capote on J.D. Salinger

Norman Mailer thinks William Burroughs is a genius, which I think is ludicrous beyond words. I don't think William Burroughs has an ounce of talent.
  Truman Capote

That's not writing, that's typing.
  Truman Capote on Jack Kerouac

Kerouac is my listening angel. Still. Even though he's dead.
  Allen Ginsberg

He had one of the more wicked minds ever going.
  Truman Capote on Mark Twain

She looks like a truck driver in drag.
  Truman Capote on Jacqueline Susann

Philip Roth is a marvelous writer but I'd hate to shake hands with him.
  Jacqueline Susann [after reading *Portnoy's Complaint*]

I'm glad there are people like Burroughs to take the dope and all so *I* don't have to do it.
  John Barth

I must say I find Martin's novels pretty difficult to get on with. It's his style. I can't even get to the end of a paragraph. It's too ornate.
  Kingsley Amis on Martin Amis

Nabokov's a real sport.
  John Barth

Nabokov graces his own novels as a figure—a figure at once majestic and ironic, the way Alfred Hitchcock appears in his own films.
  Annie Dillard

She writes like a middle-aged French *roué*. She writes like Carl Jung dreaming he is Candide.
  John Barth on Susan Sontag

He is a bad novelist and a fool. The combination usually makes for great popularity in the U.S.
  Gore Vidal on Alexander Solzhenitsyn

Who is Jorge Luis Borges?
Philip Larkin

Borges is the only living successor to Franz Kafka.
Nadine Gordimer

Updike . . . interviewed himself. That's a little too precious for my tastes.
E.L. Doctorow

His prose reminds you of the best cinematography, producing effects that are always rich, ravishing, and suspiciously frictionless.
Martin Amis on John Updike

John Updike is the Fred Astaire of American poetry.
George Garrett

There is no living writer of whom I am simply in awe, except Günter Grass.
John Irving

Erica Jong is not a human being, she's a genre.
Fran Lebowitz

Erica Jong is the Dolly Parton of American poetry.
George Garrett

I haven't read many of my contemporaries. They haven't read me either, and so we are even.
John Barth

POSTERITY

A falsehood once received from a famed writer becomes traditional to posterity.
John Dryden

Posterity—what you write for after being turned down by publishers.
George Ade

I don't care about posterity. I'm writing for today.
Kurt Weill

It's not enough to write one or two books. Posterity makes its choices from the prolific writers like Dickens and Thackeray.
Jerome Weidman

When a man is in doubt about this or that in his writing, it will often guide him if he asks himself how it will tell a hundred years hence.
Samuel Butler

To invoke one's posterity is to make a speech to maggots.
Louis-Ferdinand Céline

When writers die they become books, which is, after all, not too bad an incarnation.
Jorge Luis Borges

What I fear is not being forgotten after my death, but, rather, not being enough forgotten . . . it is not our books that survive, but our poor lives that linger in the histories.
François Mauriac

When I am dead, I hope it may be said:
"His sins were scarlet, but his books were read."
Hilaire Belloc

Posterity is as likely to be wrong as anybody else.
Heywood Broun

Posterity is just around the corner.
George S. Kaufman

INDEX OF WRITERS

INDEX

186